THE
FIELD&
STREAM

FISHING KNOTS HANDBOOK

The *Field & Stream* Fishing and Hunting Library

FISHING

HUNTING

THE
FIELD&STREAM

FISHING KNOTS HANDBOOK
Second Edition

Peter Owen

THE LYONS PRESS
Guilford, Connecticut
An imprint of The Globe Pequot Press

To buy books in quantity for corporate use
or incentives, call (800) 962-0973, ext. 4551,
or e-mail premiums@GlobePequot.com.

The Lyons Press is an imprint of The Globe Pequot Press.

10 9 8 7 6 5 4 3 2 1

Printed in the United States of America

ISBN-13: 978-1-59228-274-6
ISBN-10: 1-59228-274-1

The Library of Congress has previously cataloged an earlier
(paperback) edition as follows:

Owen, Peter, 1950–
       The field & stream fishing knots handbook / Peter Owen
              p. cm.—(Field & stream fishing and hunting library)
       Includes index.
       ISBN 1-55821-868-8
       1. Fishing knots—Handbooks, manuals, etc. I. Title. II. Title:
Field & stream fishing knots hand book. III. Series.
       SH452.9.K60934 1999
       799.1—dc21   98-54586
                                                            CIP

CONTENTS

INTRODUCTION

A fishing knot is a vital link in your tackle system. If that knot is faulty or tied incorrectly, it becomes the vulnerable weak link of the system.

Every fisherman pursues that "fish of a lifetime." Imagine when that moment finally arrives—the rush of adrenaline as the epic battle begins—and then "ping," the weak link of the system breaks, and the fish is lost through knot failure. This is just one example of how very important fishing knots are.

This book does not aim to cover every known fishing knot, but it does look in detail at the knots that have been tried and tested by generations of fishermen. If your fishing knot is tied correctly and you are fully confident with it, you have eliminated the vulnerable weak link in your tackle system.

Effective Knot Tying

Fishing knots of one kind or another have been in use for thousands of years. Since ancient times and in all societies, human beings have been devising ways of securing hooks and baits to lines. Today we can take advantage of all the imagination, ingenuity, and searching for perfection done by fishermen through the ages. We have state-of-the-art tackle, including fishing lines that are becoming more advanced through new manufacturing processes that enhance and mix different materials to formulate hybrid lines. In fact, in many of today's tackle systems, the only components that are totally reliant on the fisherman are the knots.

Effective knot tying is more than just following the instructions detailed in this book; rather, there are set, routine maneuvers that you need to implement into tying every knot. If you want to tie consistently strong and efficient knots, the following routines should become second nature to you.

• Choose your line carefully, as manufacturers produce now a wide variety of high-performance lines that best fit certain kinds of fishing and tackle. With modern advances in line material, plus the vast choice of lines available today, finding the right line for you may take a little more time, and may be a bit more costly, but it will pay off in the long run. Here is a quick overview of the lines to look for:

Nylon Monofilament

This is the standard multipurpose line that has long been a favorite because of its low memory and suppleness, making it easy to cast and handle. It has excellent knot strength and an inherent stretch that makes it forgiving when subjected to sudden strain. Still a very popular line, but it does lack some of the advanced features of today's new superlines. It doesn't have the abrasion resistance of some more advanced lines, but it is still the least expensive

Copolymer

Copolymer is a very dependable line material; it has great strength and is suitable for deep-running lures and for surface plugs and poppers. It has a finer diameter than most other lines, and good abrasion-resistance qualities, making this a great all-around line material. It has a bit of stretchiness, but not as much as monofilament.

Fluorocarbon

Fluorocarbon has been one of the great advancements in fishing tackle in recent years. It offers excellent presentation; the material is three times heavier than water so when using plugs or nymphs it gets down quicker to the desired depth, and yet when using dry flies the material leaves the fly suspended in the surface film even though the line itself sinks beneath the surface. Fluorocarbon also has the same refractive index as water, and is therefore the most invisible line available. It has a smaller diameter than standard nylon, which aids presentation and lends to superior knot strength, making flourocarbon the first choice for serious and competition anglers. Fluorocarbon isn't as flexible as some anglers might like, and its price is often higher than that of monofilament, copolymer, or braided line.

Braided lines

New, revolutionary braided lines outcast nylon many times over. These lines have no memory, allowing you to cast easier and farther, and also have no stretch, so bite detection is superb and hook set is very fast and positive. They are also about half the diameter of nylon. Many manufacturers recommend specific knots for use with braided lines, and this advice should always be followed. Two widely recommended knots are the Uni-Knot (see page 8) for hook, swivel, sinker, or lure connections, and the Double Uni-Knot (see page 42) for line-to-line connections.

• Before tying any knot, always check your line for any signs of damage. Line that is already in use can easily become damaged on rocks and snags. If you are in any doubt, safely discard that section of the line. Since monofilament line exposed to the ultraviolet light in sunlight will weaken, it is advisable to change it at least once a year, regardless.

• Before completing any knot, lubricate it with saliva or water, which helps draw it up tight and seat it correctly with a minimum of friction. Do not use a chemical lubricant, such as silicon; it may stay in the knot and increase the risk of slippage when the knot is put under tension.

• Draw the knot together slowly and evenly with a minimum of friction to ensure that it seats correctly. Some knots may have more than two ends to draw together. For example, the surgeon's knot (see page 46) must have all four ends drawn at the same time to ensure full strength.

• Continue to draw the knot together as tightly as possible. A knot will begin to slip just before it breaks—so the tighter it is drawn together, the more force it can withstand before it starts to slip. It is impossible to achieve maximum tightness with your bare hands, but the finer the gauge of line you use to tie a knot, the easier it will be to draw up tight and seat securely.

• Once the knot has been tightened and firmly seated, its end should be trimmed. Use a pair of sharp line clippers or fisherman's scissors to trim the knot ends at an angle of 45 degrees, as close to the knot as possible. It is important that the tag end does not stick out. If it extends, it can get caught up on rod rings, hooks, or weeds. Do not burn off the tag end; you could easily damage the knot and line.

All fishermen should have a pair of good-quality scissor pliers. Among their many uses are trimming knot ends, crimping lead, flattening barbs, and removing hooks. Keep them within easy reach by attaching them to a retractor secured to your fishing vest or clothing.

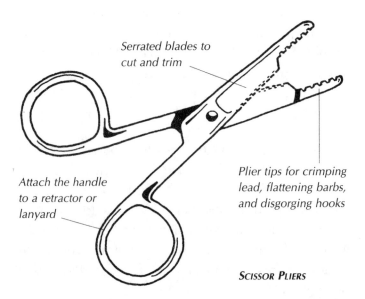

Serrated blades to cut and trim

Attach the handle to a retractor or lanyard

Plier tips for crimping lead, flattening barbs, and disgorging hooks

SCISSOR PLIERS

• Visually check your knot—good knots look good. If you are not confident that the knot has been tied and seated correctly, don't risk it! It will only take a few moments to cut it off and retie it, which is far more preferable to losing that fish of a lifetime. How a knot seats down is particularly important. Where a series of turns is involved, make sure that all the turns lie neatly shouldering each other, and that there's no slack line within the knot.

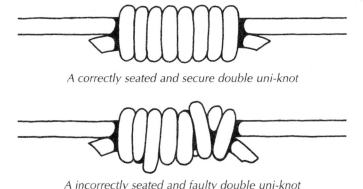

A correctly seated and secure double uni-knot

A incorrectly seated and faulty double uni-knot

• Finally… the riverbank in half light with a gale-force wind blowing is not the place to practice your knots. Practice in the comfort and ideal lighting conditions of home until your knot tying becomes second nature. Like most fishermen, you will find that you'll rely on a small number of knots to cover most situations. It is vital to be able to tie those knots quickly and confidently in any conditions.

Hooks

Tying a knot to most terminal tackle—swivels, lures, sinkers, and the like—is done by attaching the line to an eye. But this can be slightly different with hooks, because some hooks do not have eyes. In such cases, the line is knotted directly to the shank. Some knots described in this book, particularly dry-fly knots, attach the line to the shank even though the hook has an eye.

In fact, there are innumerable types, patterns, and sizes of hooks on the market today, in response to the many different methods of fishing. Here is a quick overview of the types of hooks that will affect the tying of the knots featured in this book.

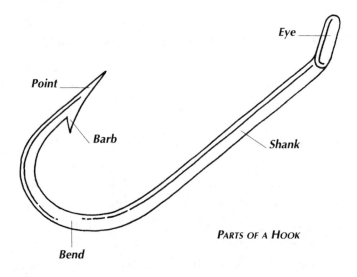

Eye

Point

Barb

Shank

PARTS OF A HOOK

Bend

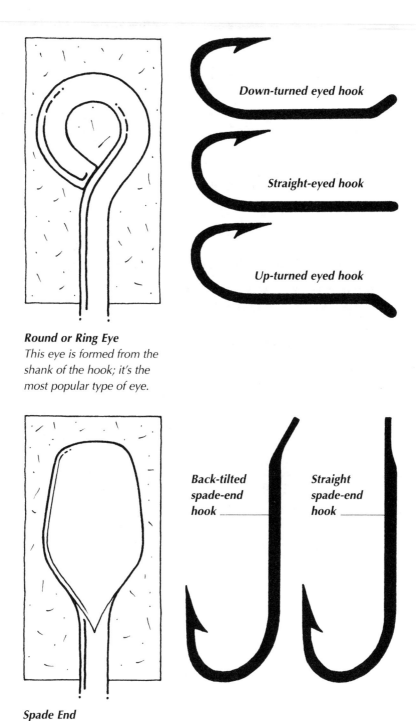

Down-turned eyed hook

Straight-eyed hook

Up-turned eyed hook

Round or Ring Eye
This eye is formed from the shank of the hook; it's the most popular type of eye.

Back-tilted spade-end hook ____

Straight spade-end hook ____

Spade End
This is formed by flattening the shank of the hook.

How to Use This Book

The step-by-step illustrations and instructions are precise, so try to follow them exactly. There are arrows to show the directions in which you should push or pull tag ends, standing parts, and loops. Reversing or changing the steps could result in defective knots.

Because of the wide variation in the types and manufacture of fishing lines, the suggested number of turns are only recommendations. A certain amount of experimentation may be required to find the optimum number of turns required for the line and knot you are using. For example, four turns may not be enough to stop your knot from slipping, rendering it defective, while six turns may prevent the knot from drawing up and seating correctly; in this case, five turns would be the optimum number.

A simple way to test knots is to tie your test knot in a separate piece of line, attach one end to a post, then, wearing a pair of strong gloves to protect your hands, pull on the other end. If you vary your pulls between a steady and a jerking action, you can test the knot under different types of strain.

Fishing Knot Terms

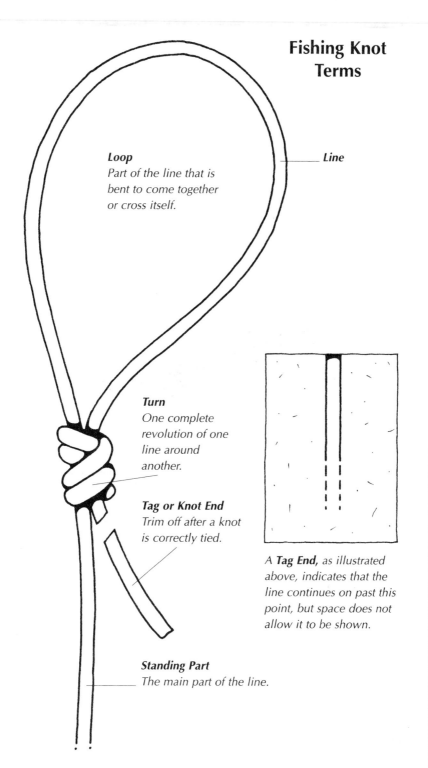

Loop
Part of the line that is
bent to come together
or cross itself.

Line

Turn
One complete
revolution of one
line around
another.

Tag or Knot End
Trim off after a knot
is correctly tied.

A **Tag End,** as illustrated
above, indicates that the
line continues on past this
point, but space does not
allow it to be shown.

Standing Part
The main part of the line.

1

HOOK AND TACKLE KNOTS

The knots in this section are for attaching hooks and flies to a leader or tippet, and attaching various items of tackle— lures, swivels, and sinkers—to a line.

An important aspect of choosing which knot to use is to feel fully confident with that knot. The knot you eventually choose will be a vital link between you and your quarry, so practice and experiment with it until you feel confident.

ARBOR KNOT

This strong but simple knot, also known as the **reel knot,** is used to secure one end of the line to the spool arbor of the reel, hence the name.

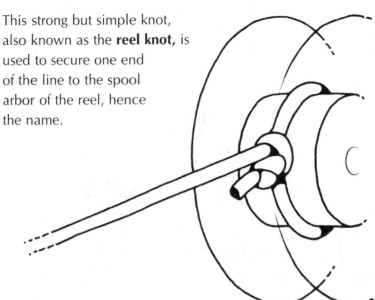

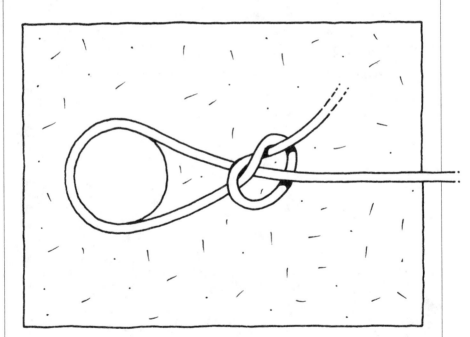

1 Take the line around the spool arbor of the reel. Then take the tag end around the standing part and tie an overhand knot.

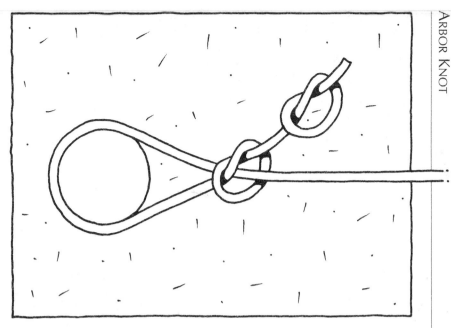

2 Tie a second overhand knot in the tag end as close as possible to the first overhand knot.

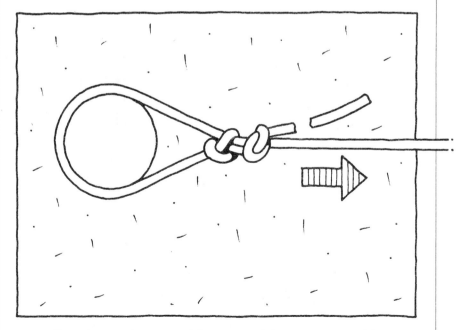

3 Pull on the standing part of the line, and the two overhand knots will jam together against the spool. Trim the knot end.

IMPROVED CLINCH KNOT

This is one of the most popular knots for tying line to a hook, fly, swivel, or lure. It is known by some fishermen as the **tucked half blood knot.** It is quick and easy to tie, and it's particularly effective with fine monofilament.

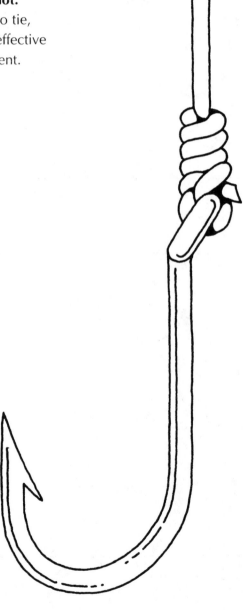

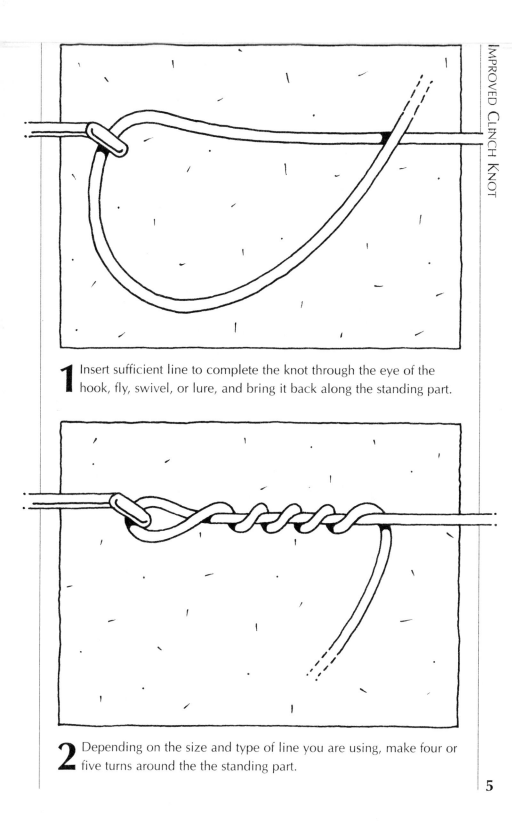

1 Insert sufficient line to complete the knot through the eye of the hook, fly, swivel, or lure, and bring it back along the standing part.

2 Depending on the size and type of line you are using, make four or five turns around the the standing part.

3 Bring the tag end back to the start and push it through the first loop created by the turns.

4 Bring the tag end back over and then push it down through the large loop.

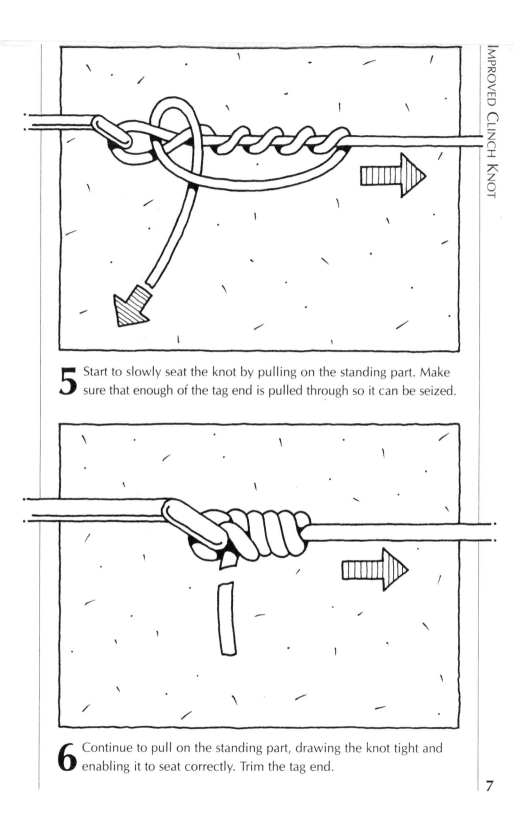

5 Start to slowly seat the knot by pulling on the standing part. Make sure that enough of the tag end is pulled through so it can be seized.

6 Continue to pull on the standing part, drawing the knot tight and enabling it to seat correctly. Trim the tag end.

UNI-KNOT

This knot, also known as the **grinner knot,** is one of the most reliable knots for tying an eyed hook or fly to a leader or tippet. It can also be used to tie line to a swivel, sinker, or lure, and is effective with most types and sizes of line.

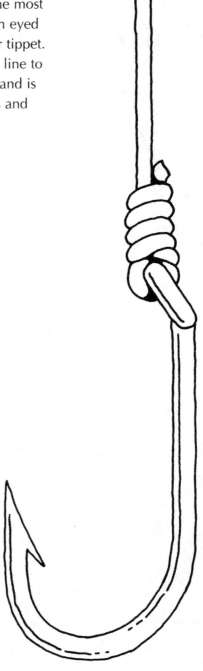

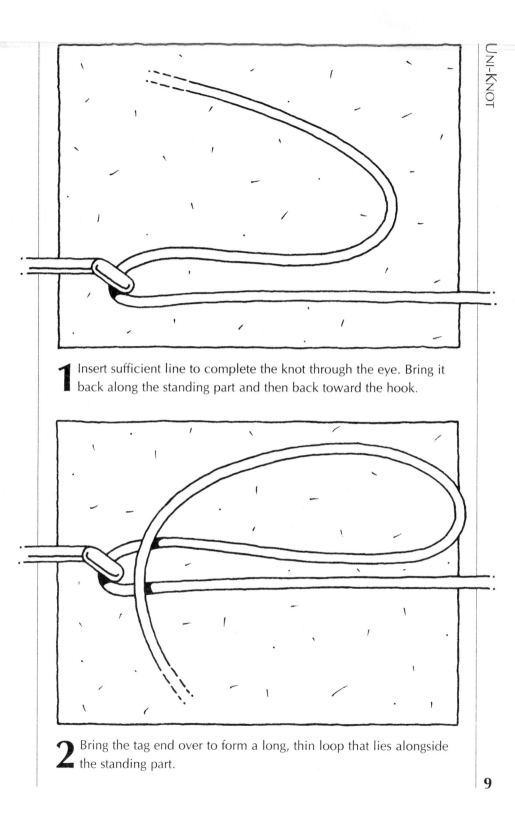

1 Insert sufficient line to complete the knot through the eye. Bring it back along the standing part and then back toward the hook.

2 Bring the tag end over to form a long, thin loop that lies alongside the standing part.

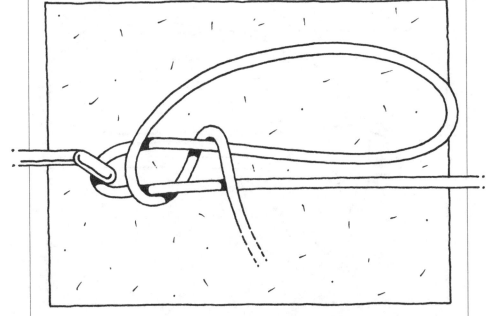

3 Bring the tag end back up behind the standing part and the lower section of the loop.

4 Bring the tag end out through the loop, to make the first turn around the standing part and the lower section of the loop.

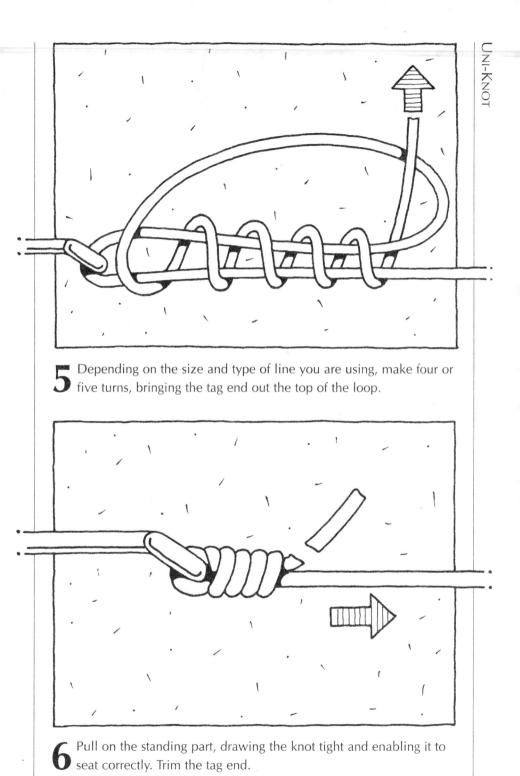

5 Depending on the size and type of line you are using, make four or five turns, bringing the tag end out the top of the loop.

6 Pull on the standing part, drawing the knot tight and enabling it to seat correctly. Trim the tag end.

11

DOUBLE TURLE KNOT

This knot is used exclusively for tying flies with up- or downturned eyes to tippets. It is not suitable for straight-eyed hooks. It is designed to allow an excellent fly presentation by keeping the fly in line with your cast.

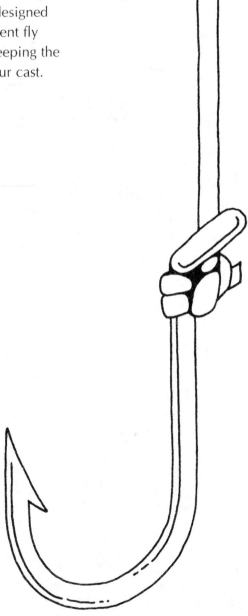

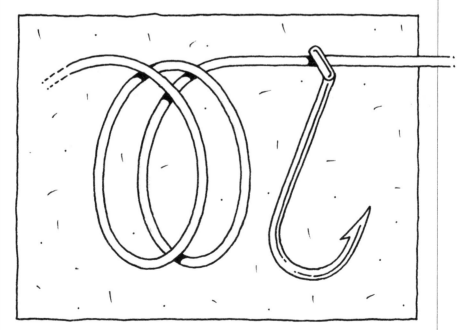

1 Insert sufficient line to complete the knot through the eye of the hook. Form a small loop.

2 Bring the tag end around to create another, identical loop. This loop sits on top of the first one.

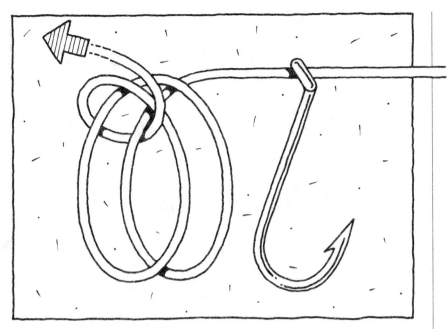

3 Continue bringing the tag end around, taking it through both loops and bringing it out at the top of the loops.

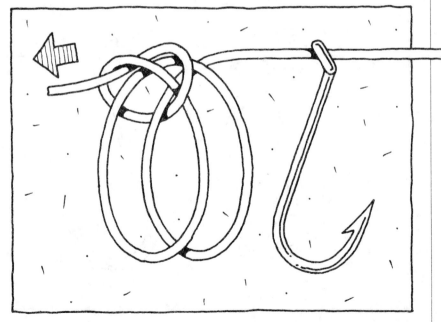

4 Tie an overhand knot around the the two loops, but don't tighten it completely. (This will allow for final adjustments.)

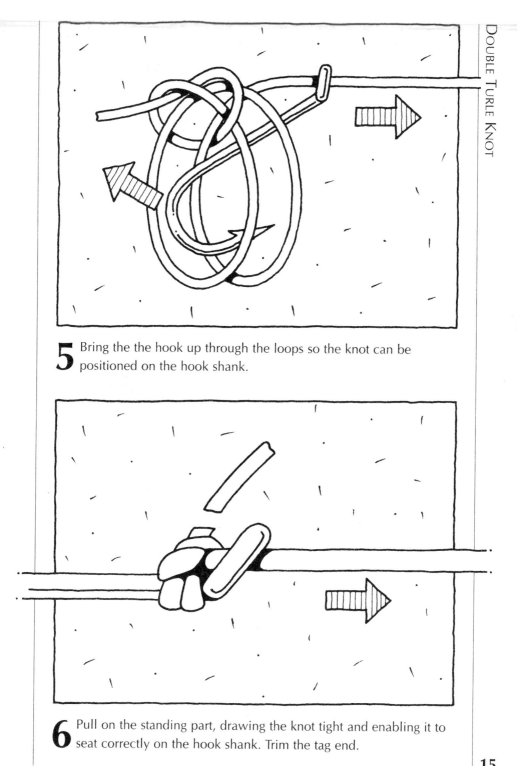

5 Bring the the hook up through the loops so the knot can be positioned on the hook shank.

6 Pull on the standing part, drawing the knot tight and enabling it to seat correctly on the hook shank. Trim the tag end.

GEORGE HARVEY DRY-FLY KNOT

Developed by fly-fishing
expert George Harvey, this
knot is specifically designed
for attaching a dry fly to a
tippet. Tied correctly, it is a
very secure knot that will
help you make a precise
and delicate dry-fly
presentation.

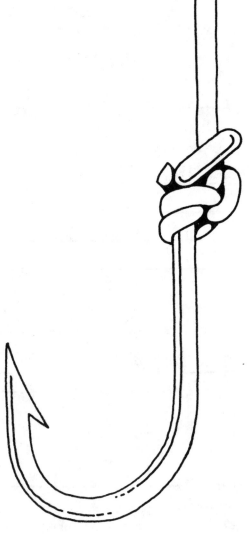

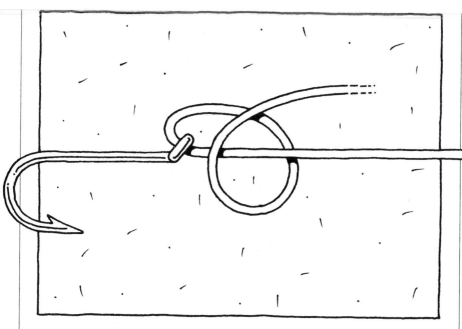

1 Insert sufficient line through the eye, and form a small circle around the standing part; the tag end should finish in front of the standing part.

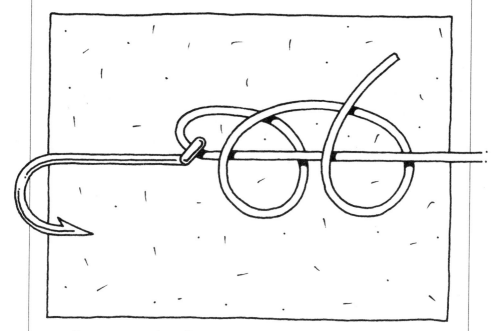

2 Create a second small circle of the same size around the standing part, again with the tag end finishing in front.

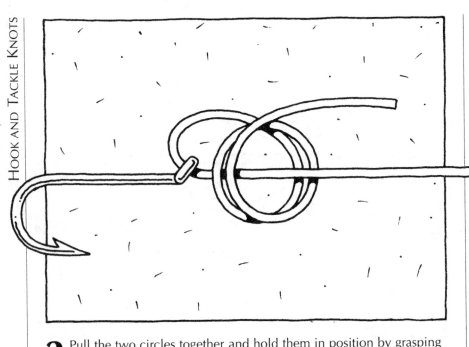

3 Pull the two circles together and hold them in position by grasping them with the standing part.

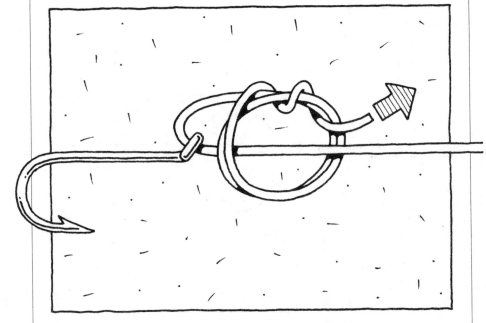

4 Loop the tag end over and through the two circles twice, bringing the tag end out in the opposite direction to the hook.

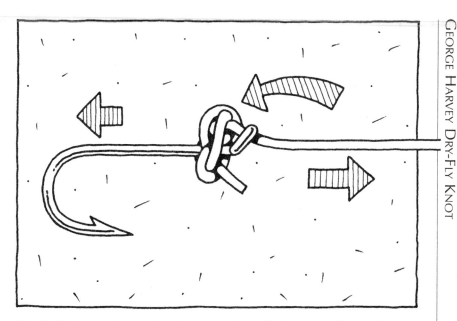

5 Hold the hook and slowly start to draw the knot tight by pulling on the standing part. If the knot is tied correctly, the loops will slide back and jump over the eye of the hook as it is drawn up.

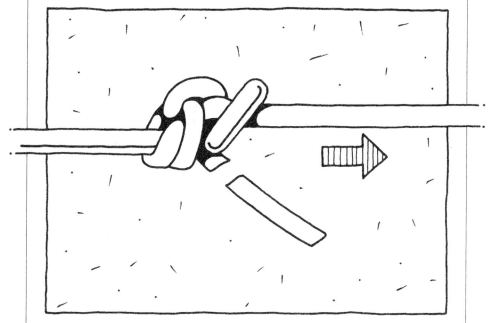

6 Continue to pull on the standing part, drawing the knot tight and enabling it to seat correctly. Trim the tag end.

NONSLIP MONO KNOT

This knot is designed to give artificial lures a more attractive action in the water. The knot forms a loop that doesn't slip, and allows the lure to move around more. The number of turns required when tying this knot will differ with various types and sizes of line. Try seven turns for fine monofilament, fewer turns with heavier line.

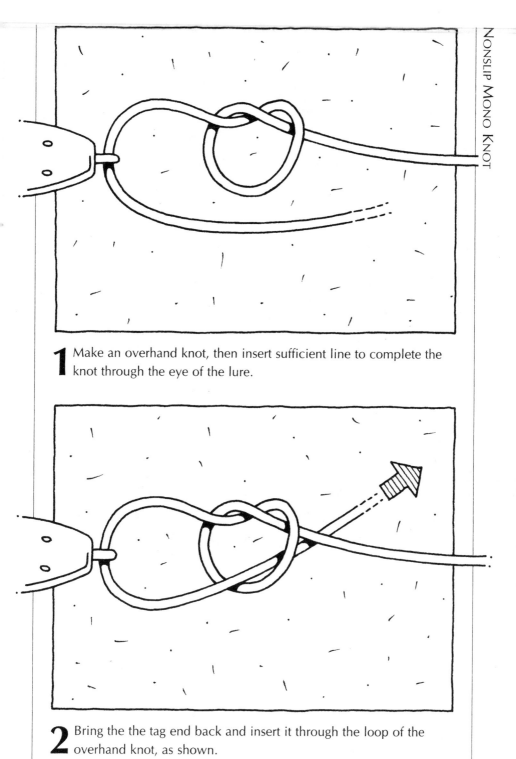

1 Make an overhand knot, then insert sufficient line to complete the knot through the eye of the lure.

2 Bring the the tag end back and insert it through the loop of the overhand knot, as shown.

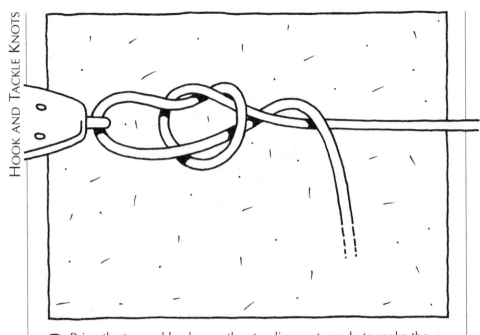

3 Bring the tag end back over the standing part, ready to make the required number of turns.

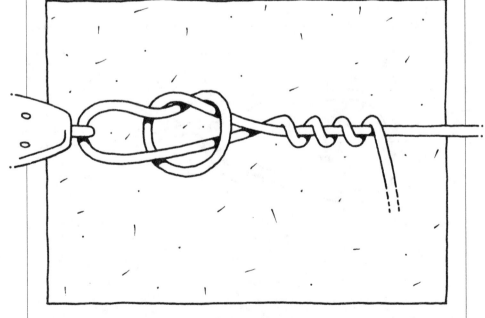

4 Depending on the size and type of line you are using, make the required number of turns.

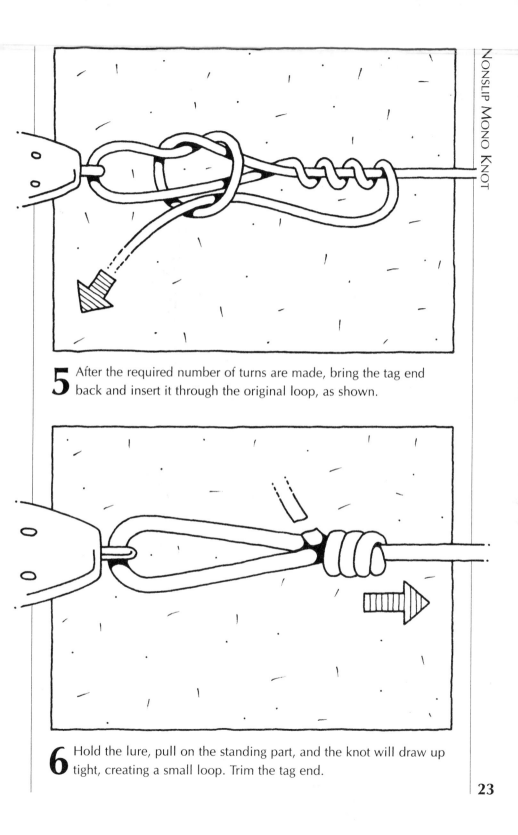

5 After the required number of turns are made, bring the tag end back and insert it through the original loop, as shown.

6 Hold the lure, pull on the standing part, and the knot will draw up tight, creating a small loop. Trim the tag end.

PALOMAR KNOT

This is a quick and effective
knot for tying onto swivels,
lures, and sinkers. It uses
more line than other knots;
allow for this when tying.

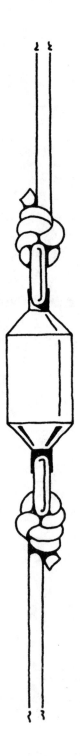

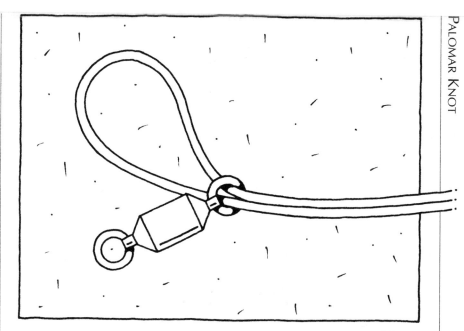

1 Insert a loop of sufficient double line to complete the knot through the eye of the swivel, lure, or sinker.

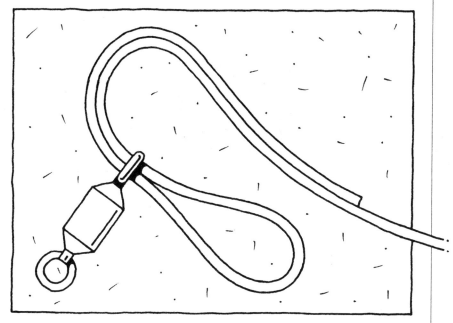

2 Bring the loop and swivel, lure, or sinker back alongside the standing part.

25

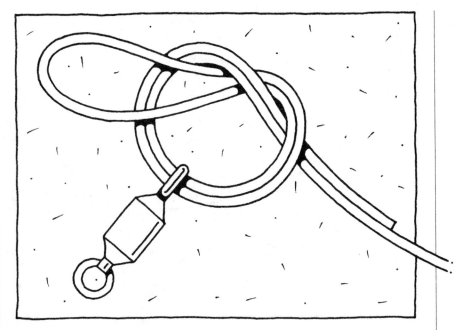

3 Bring the loop around and make an overhand knot, as shown above.

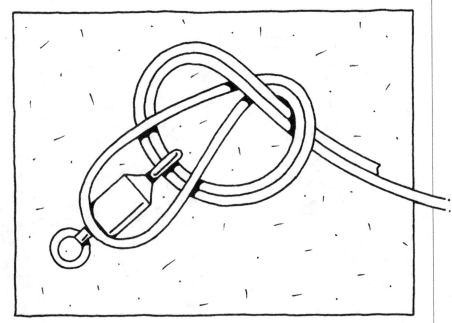

4 Bring the loop back down and position it over the top of the swivel, lure, or sinker.

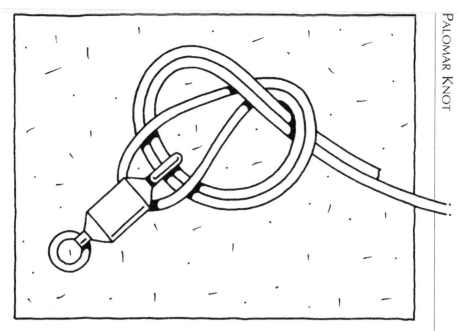

5 Hold the tag end and the standing part together, and pull the swivel, lure, or sinker out through the loop.

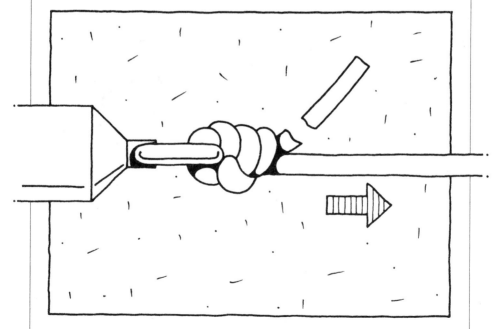

6 Pull on the standing part and the tag end together, drawing the knot tight and enabling it to seat correctly. Trim the tag end.

27

SNELLING AN EYED HOOK

The snell is still widely used
by saltwater fishermen, but
is often overlooked by other
anglers. Tied correctly, it is a
very secure knot for attaching
an eyed hook to a line.

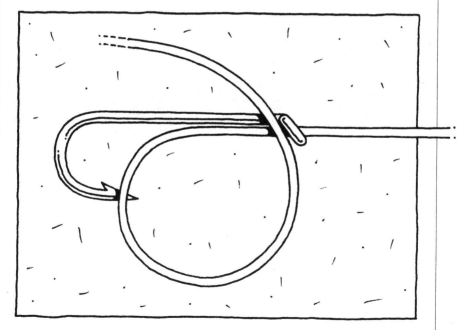

1 Insert sufficient line to complete the knot through the eye, and then turn it back in the direction of the standing part.

2 Bring the tag end up to form a large loop. This loop needs to lie along the hook shank.

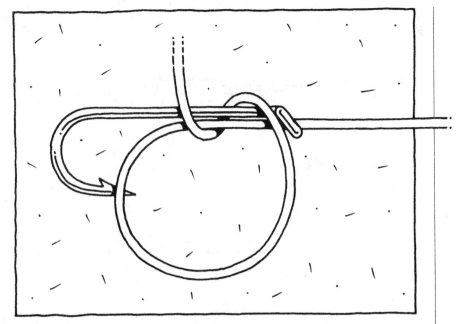

3 Bring the tag end down to create the first turn around the loop and the hook shank.

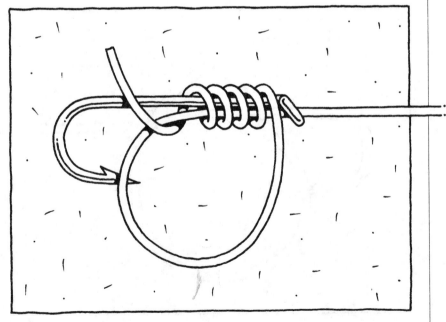

4 Depending on the size and type of line you are using, make five or six turns away from the hook eye toward the hook point.

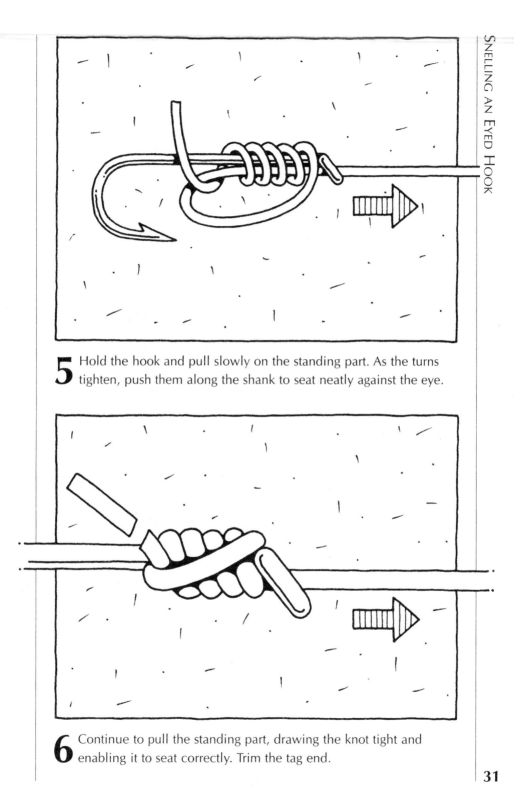

5 Hold the hook and pull slowly on the standing part. As the turns tighten, push them along the shank to seat neatly against the eye.

6 Continue to pull the standing part, drawing the knot tight and enabling it to seat correctly. Trim the tag end.

SPADE-END KNOT

Still a popular alternative to an eyed hook is the spade-end hook. This knot is designed specifically for tying this type of hook to a line. Take care to seat the knot correctly around the hook shank.

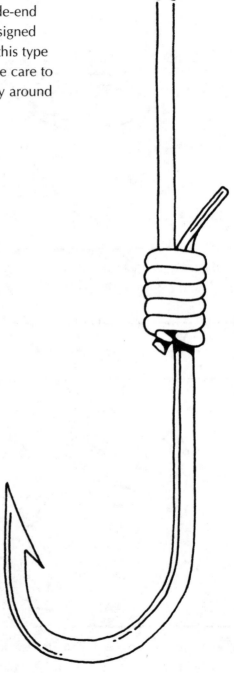

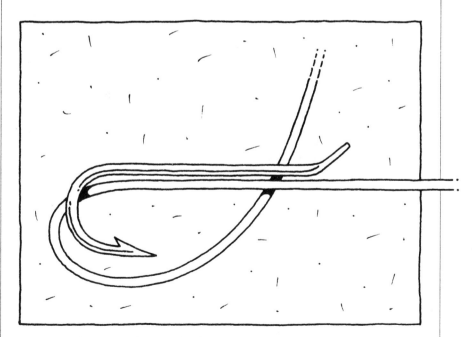

1 Place sufficient line to complete the knot alongside the shank of the hook, and bring the tag end back toward the standing part.

2 Bring the tag end up and behind the hook shank and standing part to form a large loop.

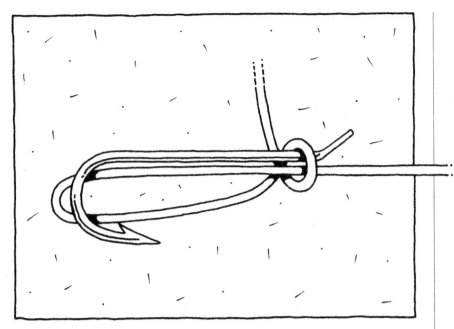

3 Bring the tag end over to form the first turn. This first turn also tightens the standing part and the loop against the hook shank.

4 Depending on the size and type of line you are using, make five or six turns away from the spade end, and bring the tag end out of the loop.

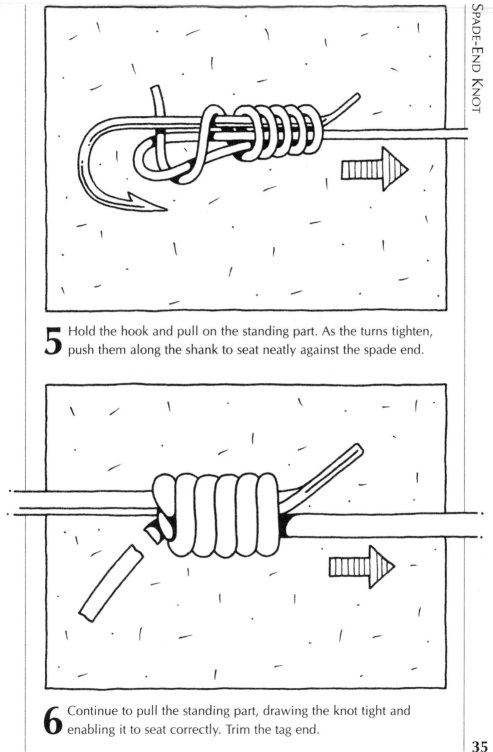

5 Hold the hook and pull on the standing part. As the turns tighten, push them along the shank to seat neatly against the spade end.

6 Continue to pull the standing part, drawing the knot tight and enabling it to seat correctly. Trim the tag end.

2

JOINING
LINES

The joining of two lines is one of the most important connections in a tackle system.

The four tested and reliable knots in this section, when correctly tied, will provide secure connections. Because of the wide variety of line materials and sizes available, the number of turns required in each knot will differ. A general guideline is given, but a certain amount of experimentation may be required for you to achieve the optimum number of turns.

BLOOD KNOT

This longtime favorite fishing knot is still one of the most effective ways to join two lines, especially monofilament lines that are of the same or similar diameters. Having an equal number of turns on both sides of the knot helps absorb strain and shock.

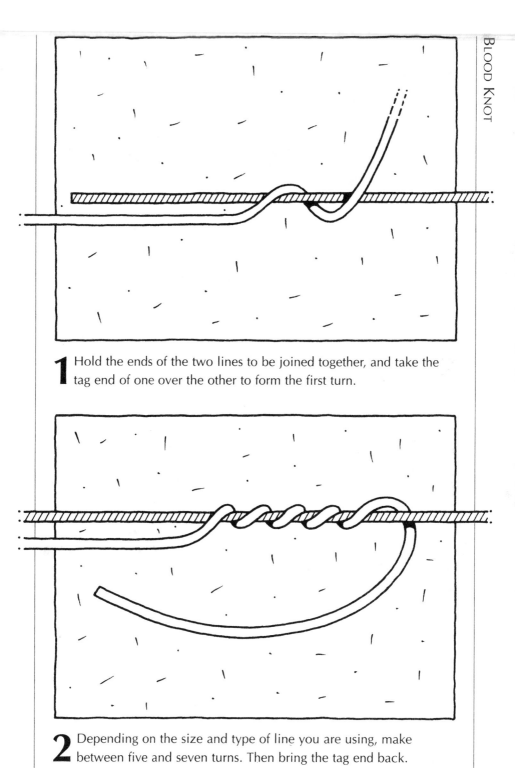

1 Hold the ends of the two lines to be joined together, and take the tag end of one over the other to form the first turn.

2 Depending on the size and type of line you are using, make between five and seven turns. Then bring the tag end back.

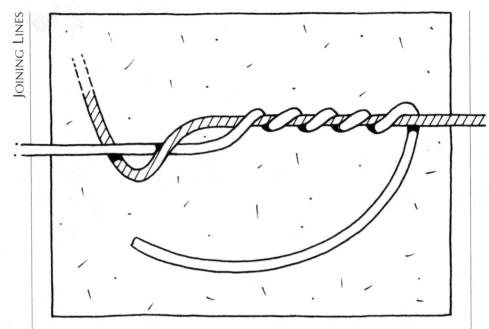

3 Holding the lines and turns in position, take the tag end of the other line and start to make a turn, as shown.

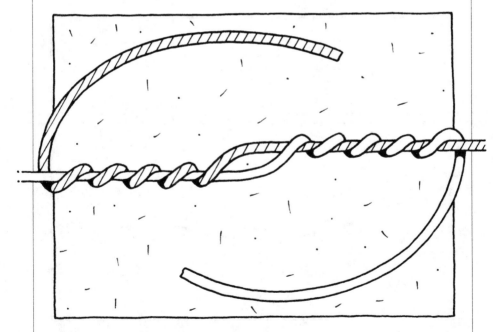

4 Make an equal number of turns, taking care to leave a clear division between the two sets of turns.

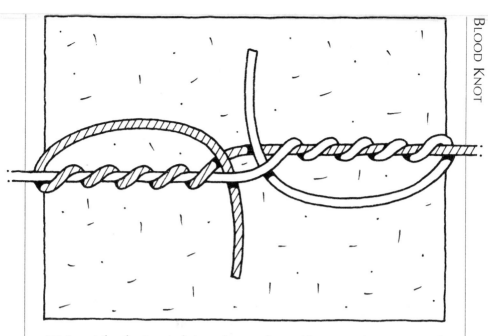

5 Insert the the tag ends into the gap formed between the two sets of turns, one going up, the other going down, as shown.

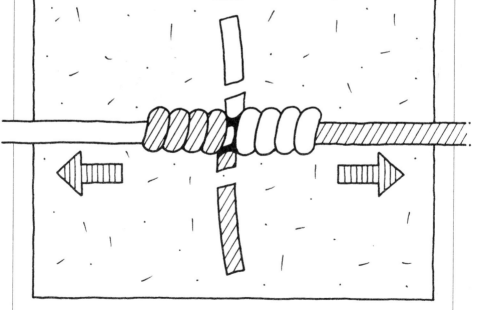

6 Slowly pull the two standing parts and tag ends until the knot seats correctly with the tag ends seized in the center. Trim the tag ends.

DOUBLE UNI-KNOT

Also known as the **double grinner knot,** this knot uses the tying principle of two knots tied back to back and then seated together to form a strong connection. With practice, it is easy to tie and very effective.

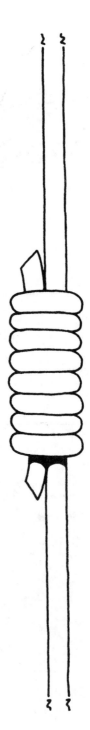

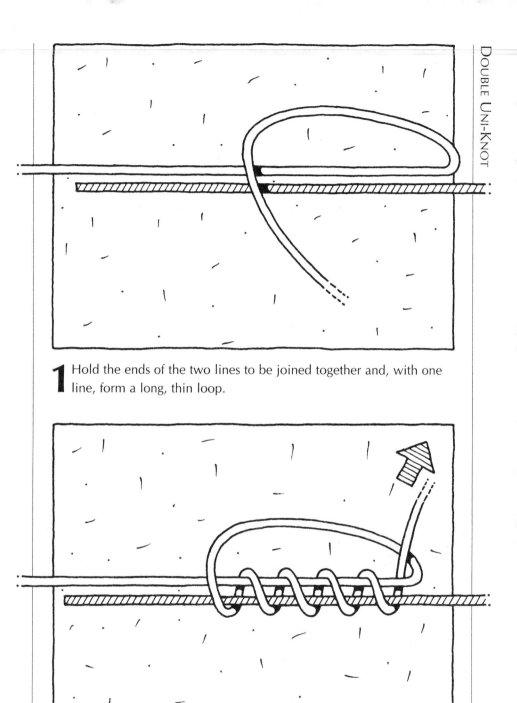

1 Hold the ends of the two lines to be joined together and, with one line, form a long, thin loop.

2 Depending on the size and type of line, make five to seven turns around both lines, bringing the tag end out the end of the loop.

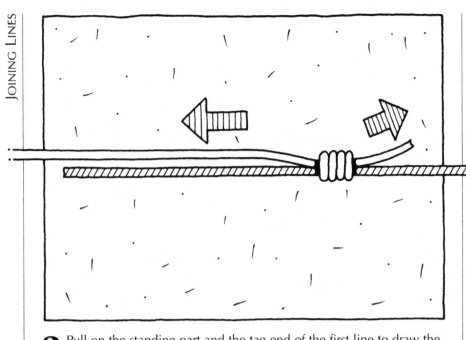

3 Pull on the standing part and the tag end of the first line to draw the knot together. Do not draw the knot completely tight at this stage.

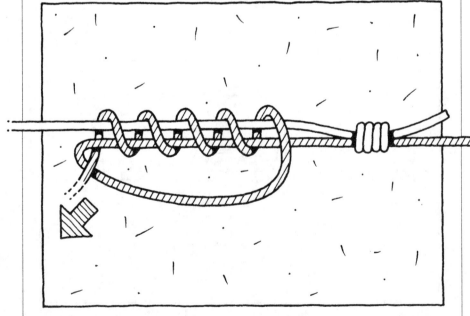

4 With the second line, create a knot identical to the one you created with the first line, except the other way around.

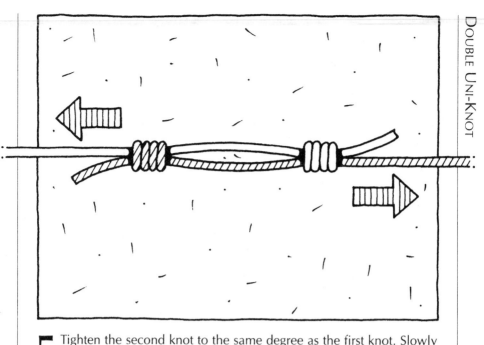

5 Tighten the second knot to the same degree as the first knot. Slowly pull on both standing parts to bring the knots together.

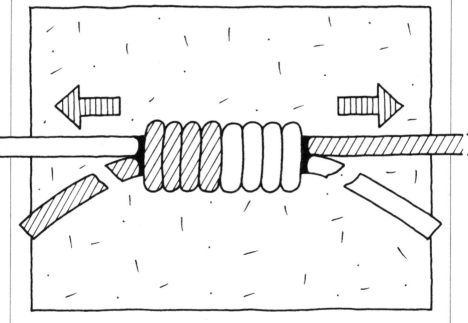

6 Continue to pull on both standing parts until the two knots seat together, and the complete knot is drawn tight. Trim the tag ends.

45

SURGEON'S KNOT

Also known as the **water knot,**
this is one of the best all-around
knots for joining two lines. The
lines need to be of the same or
similar diameters and types for
this knot to be effective. If you
find it difficult to tie from the
diagrams, just remember that
one of the lines—in most
cases the leader—needs to
be short enough to pass
through the loop.

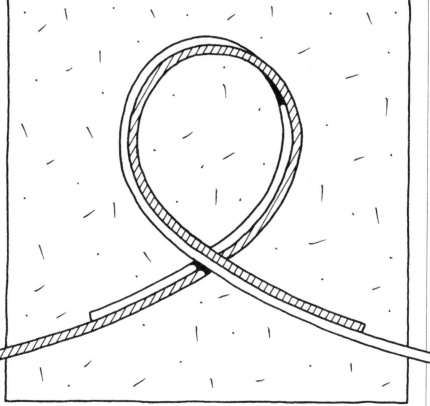

1 Hold sufficient lengths of the two lines side by side. In the illustration above, the unshaded clear line is the shorter one.

2 Hold both lines together and twist them over to form an open loop, as shown above.

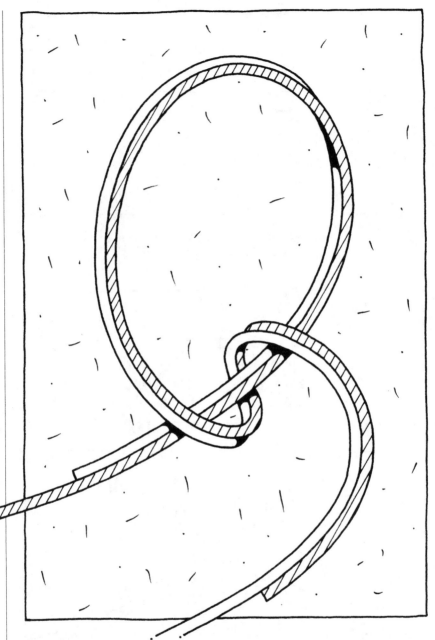

3 Make a first turn as shown. The unshaded clear line is short enough to pass through the loop. It is important to keep the loop open at this stage in order to make more turns.

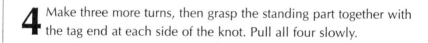

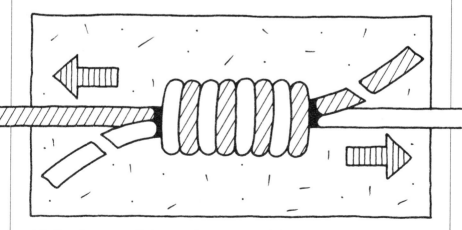

4 Make three more turns, then grasp the standing part together with the tag end at each side of the knot. Pull all four slowly.

5 Continue to pull the standing parts and the tag ends, drawing the knot tight and enabling it to seat correctly. Trim the tag ends.

ALBRIGHT KNOT

This is one of the most reliable fishing knots for joining two lines of unequal diameters and different materials. A good time to use this knot, for example, is when you're connecting monofilament backing to a fly line.

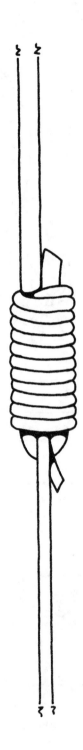

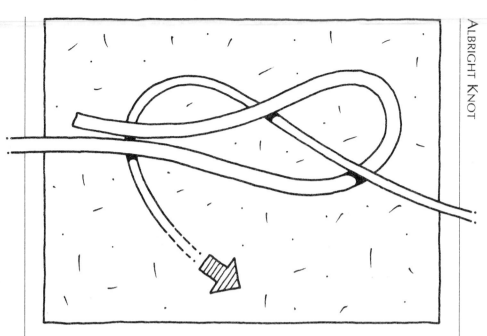

1 Create a loop in the tag end of the heavier line, then feed the tag end of the lighter line through the loop.

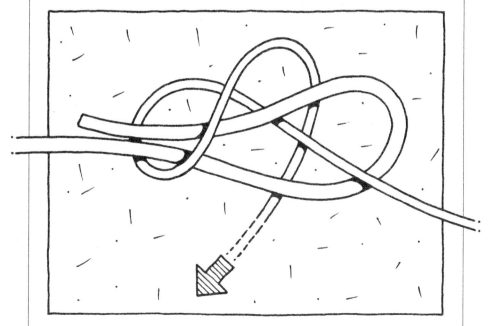

2 Bring the tag end up and over the loop to create the first turn, as shown above.

51

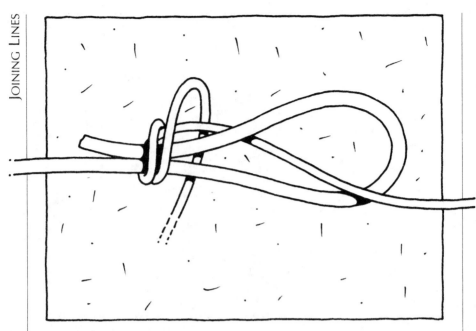

3 Make a series of turns around all three strands from left to right. Keep the turns as tight as possible.

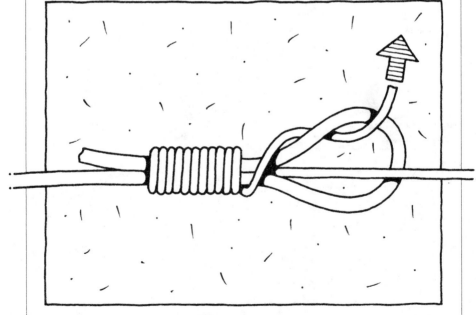

4 Depending on the size and type of line, make a minimum of 10 turns, bringing the tag end out the end of the heavier line's loop.

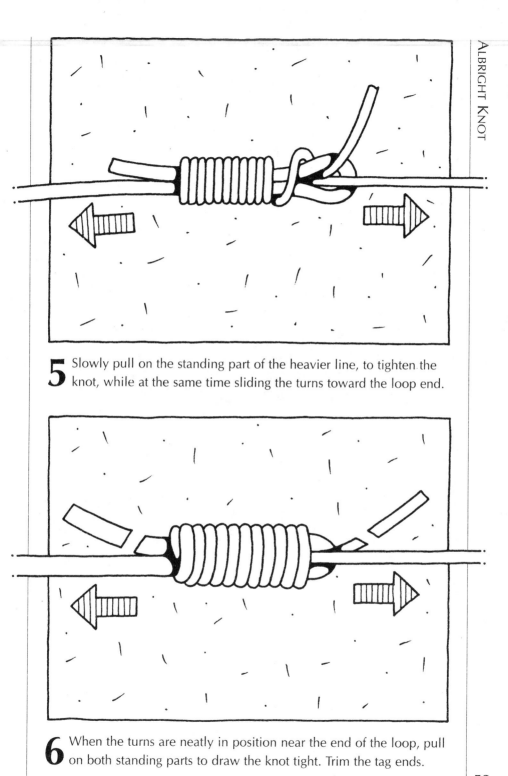

5 Slowly pull on the standing part of the heavier line, to tighten the knot, while at the same time sliding the turns toward the loop end.

6 When the turns are neatly in position near the end of the loop, pull on both standing parts to draw the knot tight. Trim the tag ends.

3
LOOPS

Correctly tied loops are exceptionally strong, and for many anglers the interlocking-loop system (see page 56) is an integral part of the tackle system.

Loops have a wide range of fishing applications, and the interlocking-loop system provides the perfect answer for any line connection that needs to be changed frequently. A good example is being able to change a premade leader quickly and efficiently while fishing. Because no actual knot tying is involved, this can be a real advantage in adverse weather conditions or poor light.

SURGEON'S LOOP

This reliable and widely used loop uses the same tying method as the surgeon's knot (see page 46), except it is constructed from a single length of line. It is also known as the **double loop.**

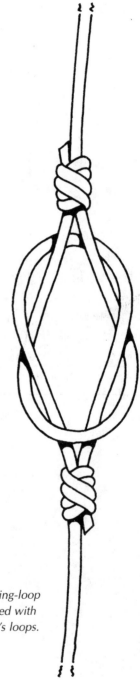

An interlocking-loop system created with two surgeon's loops.

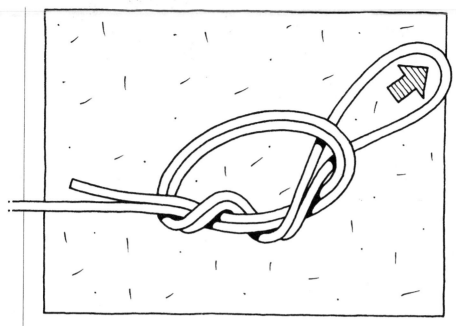

1 Double the tag end of a length of line, create a double overhand knot as shown above, and then slowly pull the loop through.

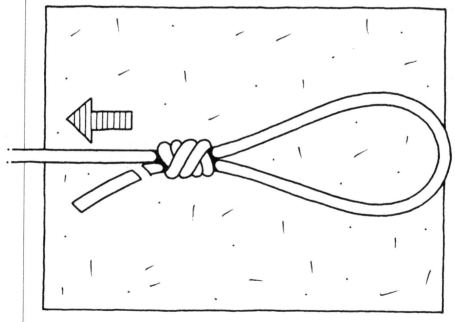

2 Finalize the size of the loop required, then draw the knot tight by holding the loop and pulling the standing part. Trim the tag end.

DROPPER LOOP

This extremely useful loop is used by a wide range of anglers; to many, it is known as the **blood loop**. It creates a loop at right angles to the main line. Fly fishermen use it to attach additional flies, known as droppers, while other anglers use it to attach sinkers and extra hooks to a line.

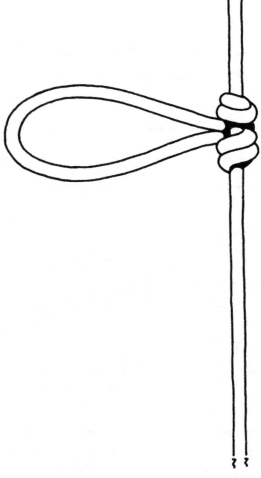

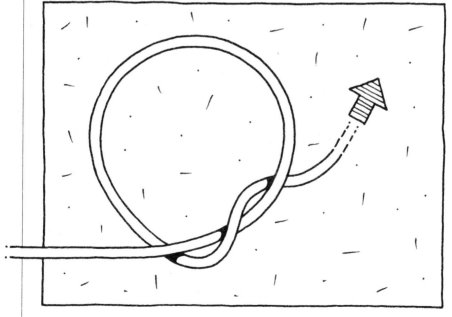

1 Choose the point in the line at which you want to position your dropper loop, and form a circle.

2 The size of the circle will determine the size of your dropper loop. Create the first turn with an overhand knot.

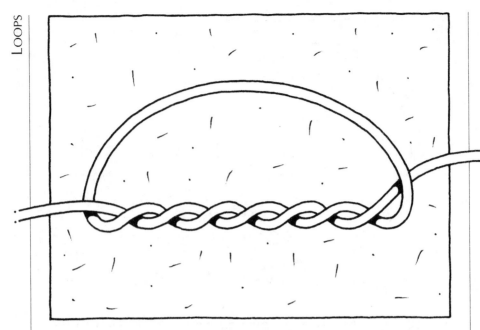

3 Depending on the size and type of line, make three or four turns in total, and position the knot as shown above.

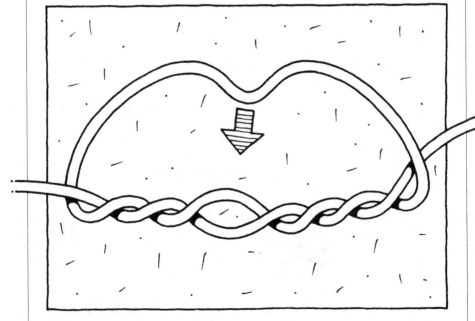

4 Create a slightly larger gap in the center of the turns, and bring the top of the main loop down to form the dropper loop.

5 Form the dropper loop, then pull it down as far as possible through the gap in the center of the turns.

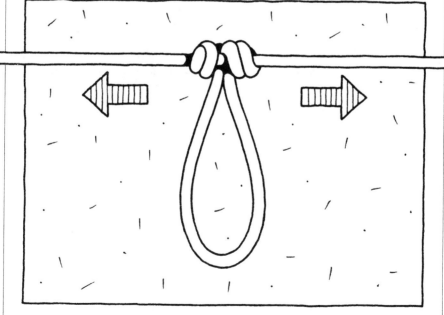

6 Pull both standing parts at the same time to tighten the knot. The loop will form itself; it is not necessary to pull it.

PERFECTION LOOP

This knot creates a very strong
and reliable end loop; leaders
and tippets can be easily
attached to it.

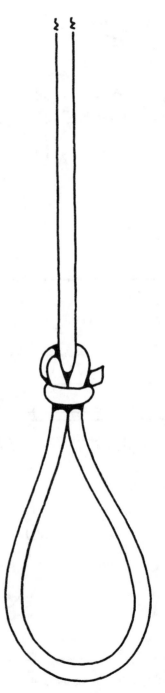

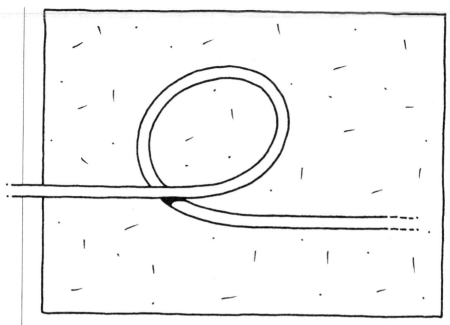

1 Create a loop near the end of the line, as shown, then hold that loop in position.

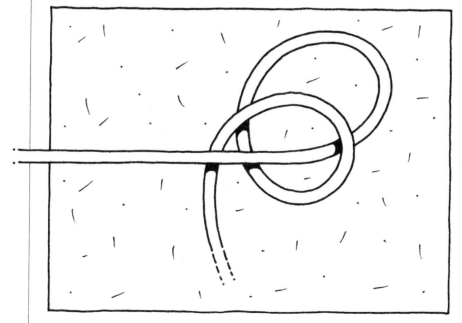

2 Bring the tag end back over to form a second loop. The tag end should now be positioned behind the standing part.

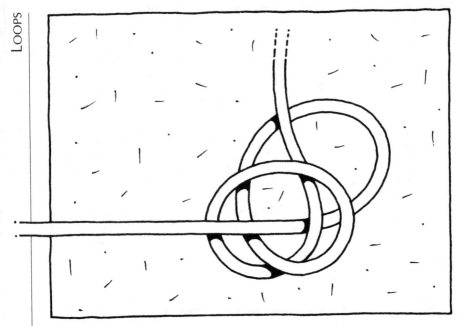

3 Bring the tag end back up and position it between the two loops, as shown above.

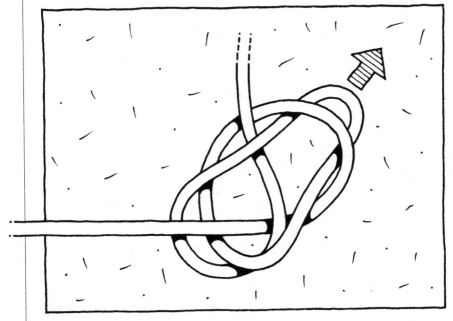

4 Grasp the front loop, form it into a narrower loop, and then push it through the rear loop.

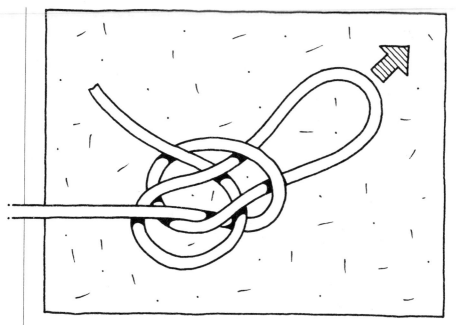

5 Pull the loop through as far as possible. You can still adjust the size of the loop at this stage, if desired.

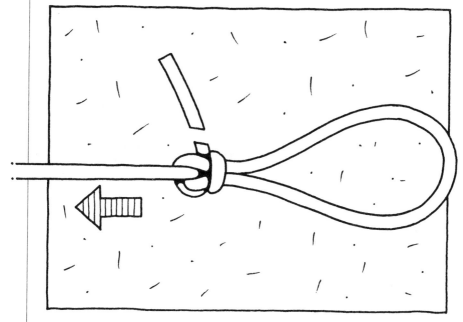

6 Hold the loop and pull the standing part, drawing the knot tight and enabling it to seat correctly. Trim the tag end.

BIMINI TWIST

This knot creates a loop that will give 100 percent knot strength. It is tied at the tag end of the line to form a main connection that other line or tackle can be secured to. It may take a little time to perfect, but once mastered, it provides one of the most secure loops possible.

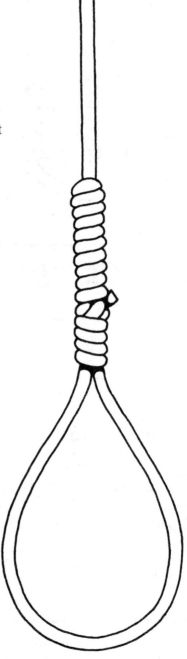

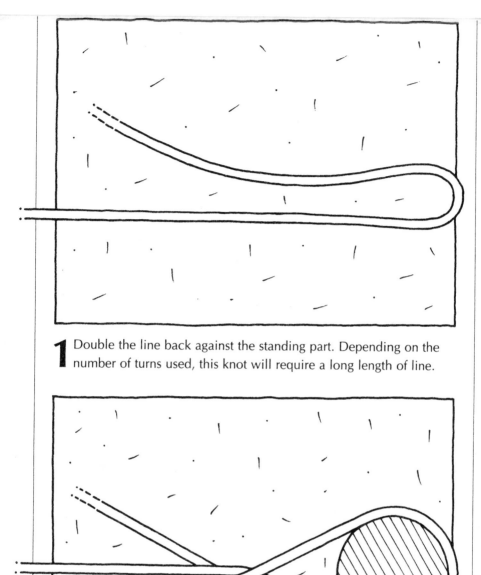

1 Double the line back against the standing part. Depending on the number of turns used, this knot will require a long length of line.

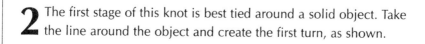

2 The first stage of this knot is best tied around a solid object. Take the line around the object and create the first turn, as shown.

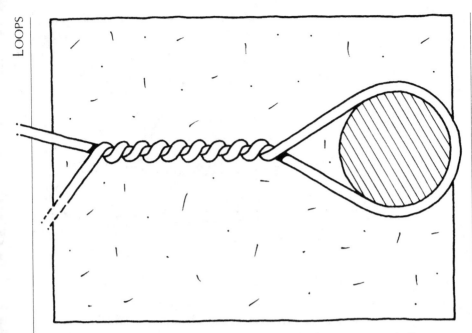

3 Depending on the line you're using, make between 8 and 20 turns. Fifteen turns are recommended for regular monofilament.

4 It is very important to keep pressure on both the standing part and the tag end, to keep the turns as tight as possible.

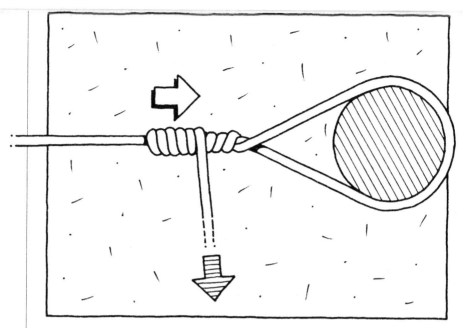

5 Make approximately the same number of turns back over the original turns in the direction of the solid object.

6 At this point, remove the loop from the solid object, and create a holding knot with the tag end.

7 Still keeping pressure on the standing part and the loop, tighten the holding knot and bring the tag end out.

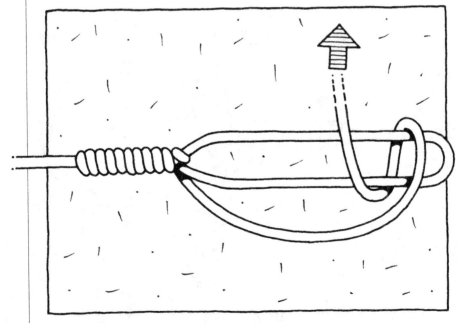

8 Holding the knot in the position shown above, make a turn around the narrowed loop with the tag end.

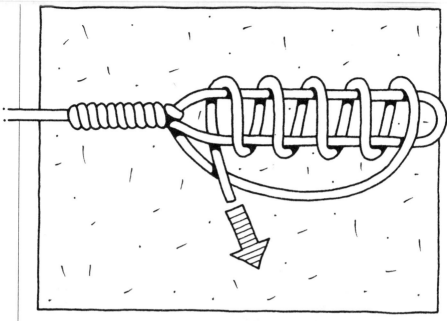

9 Make four or five turns, and then pull slowly on the tag end to seat this series of turns back against the original turns.

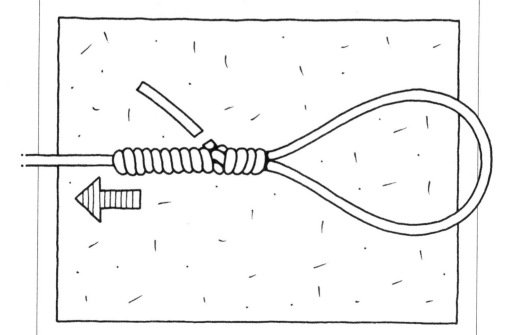

10 With the second series of turns seated correctly, hold the loop and pull the standing part to finalize the knot. Trim the tag end.

4
FLY-LINE
KNOTS

A fly line requires a secure knot at both ends—to attach the backing line at one end, and to attach the butt section of the leader at the other.

This section covers various methods of tying these knots, some of which can initially prove difficult. Follow the instructions closely and practice before tying the final knot. If you are not totally confident with your knots, seek help from your local tackle store. In most cases, the owner will be only too pleased to help out.

NAIL KNOT

This knot is used to attach
backing line or a leader to
a fly line. It is tied with
assistance of a small-diameter
nail or needle. The nail or
needle acts to stiffen the fly
line and help form the knot.

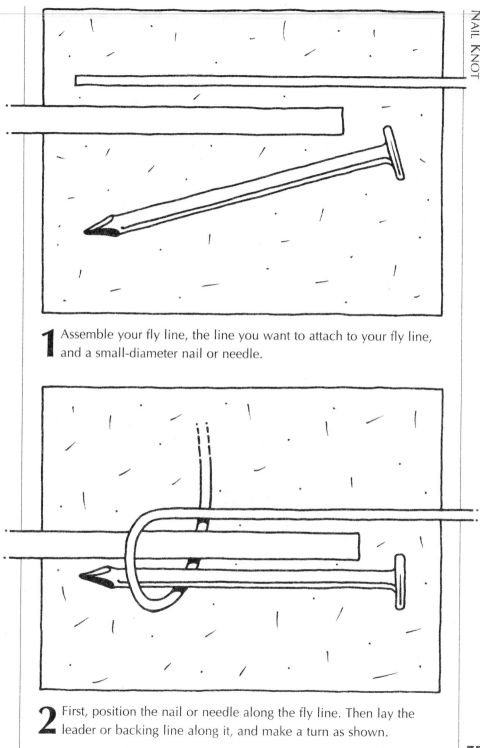

1 Assemble your fly line, the line you want to attach to your fly line, and a small-diameter nail or needle.

2 First, position the nail or needle along the fly line. Then lay the leader or backing line along it, and make a turn as shown.

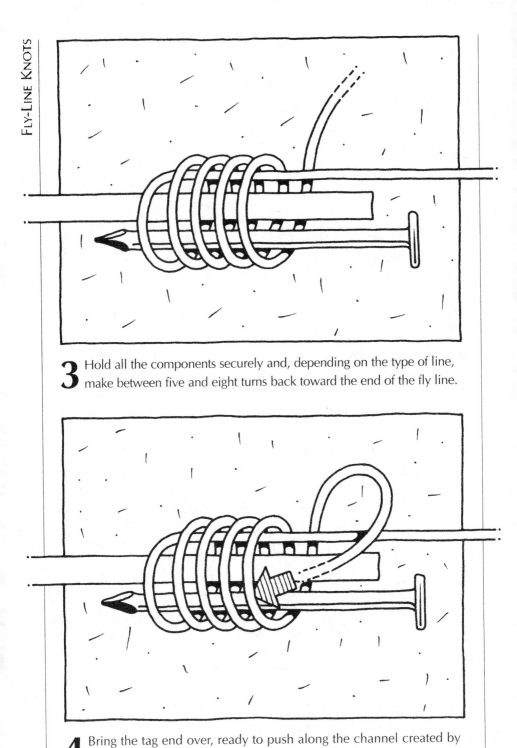

3 Hold all the components securely and, depending on the type of line, make between five and eight turns back toward the end of the fly line.

4 Bring the tag end over, ready to push along the channel created by the nail or needle.

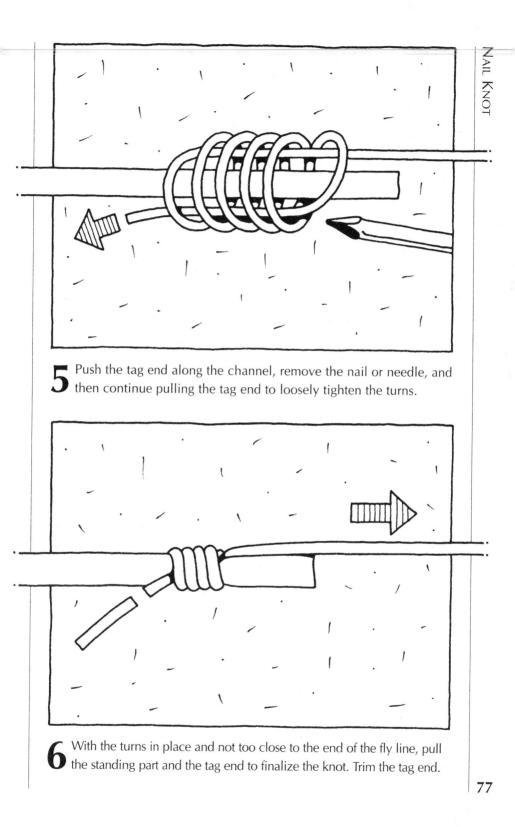

5 Push the tag end along the channel, remove the nail or needle, and then continue pulling the tag end to loosely tighten the turns.

6 With the turns in place and not too close to the end of the fly line, pull the standing part and the tag end to finalize the knot. Trim the tag end.

NEEDLE KNOT

This knot creates the best solution for joining a monofilament leader to a fly line. It is a very neat and smooth connection that is extremely strong. It will not snag on rod guides, or pick up debris in the water.

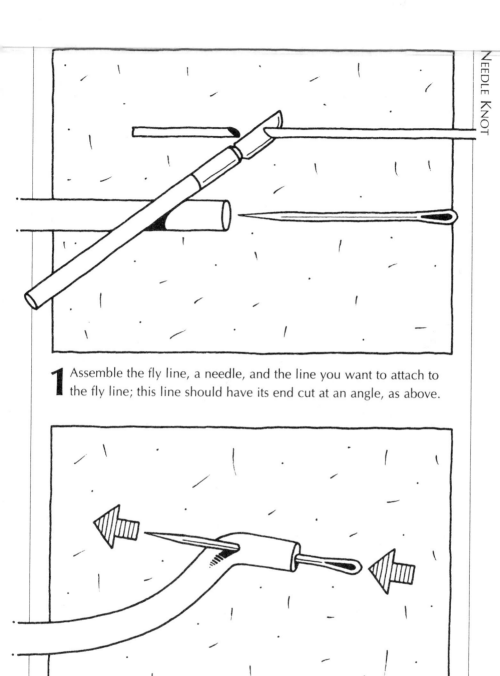

1 Assemble the fly line, a needle, and the line you want to attach to the fly line; this line should have its end cut at an angle, as above.

2 Push the needle along the center of the fly line, and then bend the fly line to allow the needle to exit.

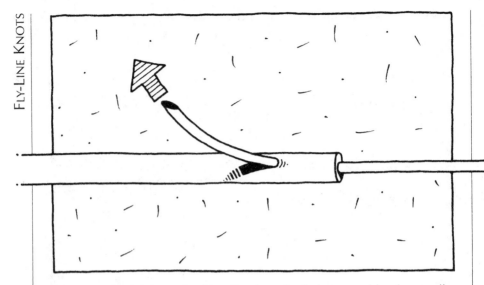

3 Insert the leader or backing line into the hole created by the needle and then out the hole in the side of the fly line. Should it prove difficult to insert the leader or backing line, replace the needle, heat its point, and then remove. The heated needle point will open the hole; take care to not damage the lines with excess heat.

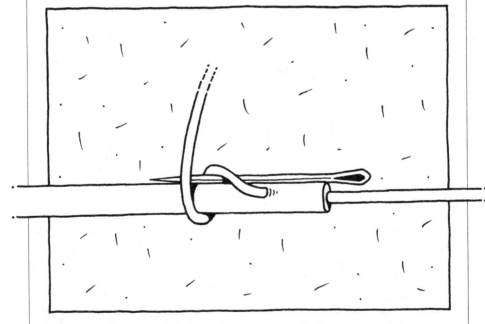

4 Position the needle along the side of the fly line, and make a turn with the tag end of the leader or backing line.

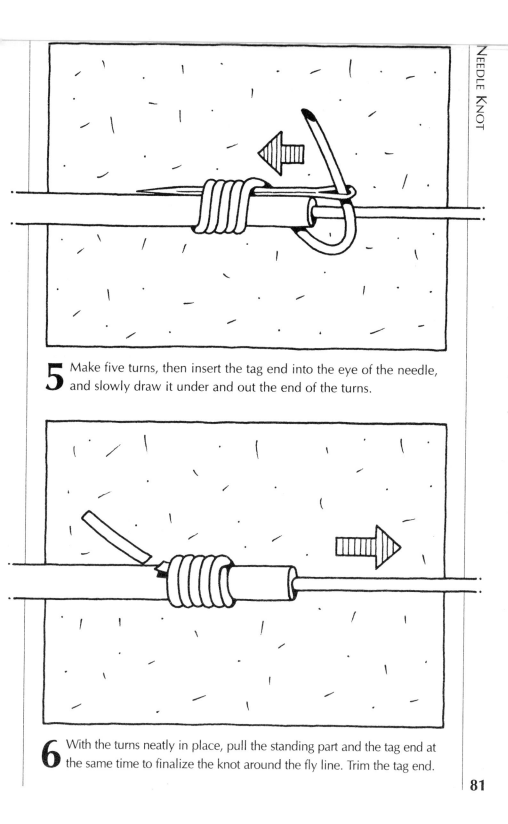

5 Make five turns, then insert the tag end into the eye of the needle, and slowly draw it under and out the end of the turns.

6 With the turns neatly in place, pull the standing part and the tag end at the same time to finalize the knot around the fly line. Trim the tag end.

NEEDLE MONO LOOP

This is a good alternative to the needle knot (see page 78) if you prefer a loop at the end of your fly line to make interlocking-loop connections. The tying method is the same as for the needle knot, except you use a doubled monofilament line.

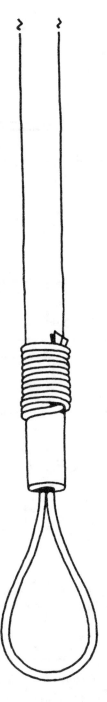

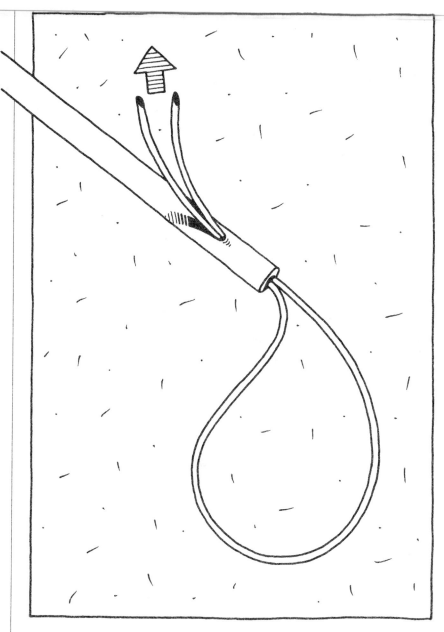

1 Create the hole in the fly line in exactly the same way as the needle knot (see pages 79 and 80). But instead of inserting a single piece of line, insert a piece of line that has been doubled to form a loop at the end of the fly line. Determine the size of loop you require at this stage.

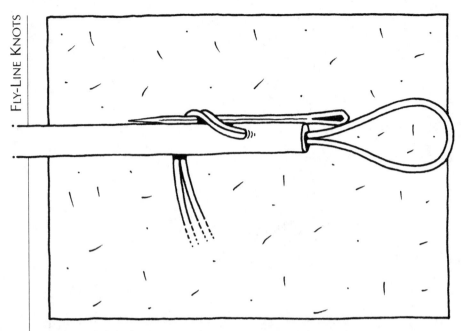

3 With the size of the loop determined, lay the needle along the fly line and start to make the first turn with the two strands of line.

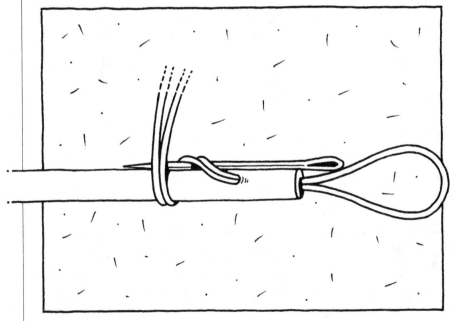

4 Continue the first turn. Because two strands of line are being used, it is important that all the strands seat tightly against each other.

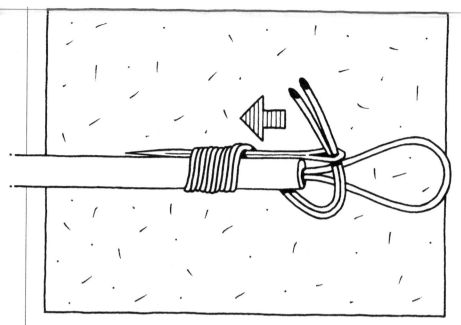

5 Make three to five turns, then insert the tag ends into the eye of the needle, and slowly draw them under and out of the end of the turns.

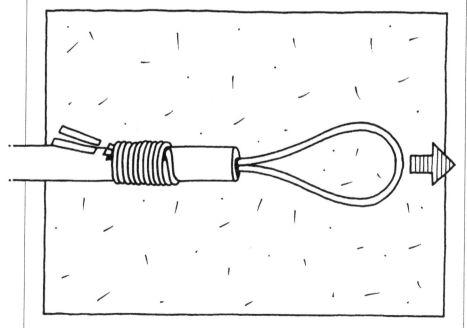

6 With the turns neatly in place, pull the loop and the tag ends at the same time to finalize the knot around the fly line. Trim the tag ends.

85

TUBE NAIL/NEEDLE KNOT

If you find tying the nail knot
(see page 74) or the needle
knot (see page 78) difficult,
substitute a small, hollow tube
for the nail or needle. The
tube will need to be stiff
enough to provide support to
the fly line while you form the
knot, and wide enough to be
able to pass the line through.

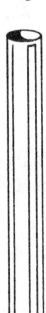

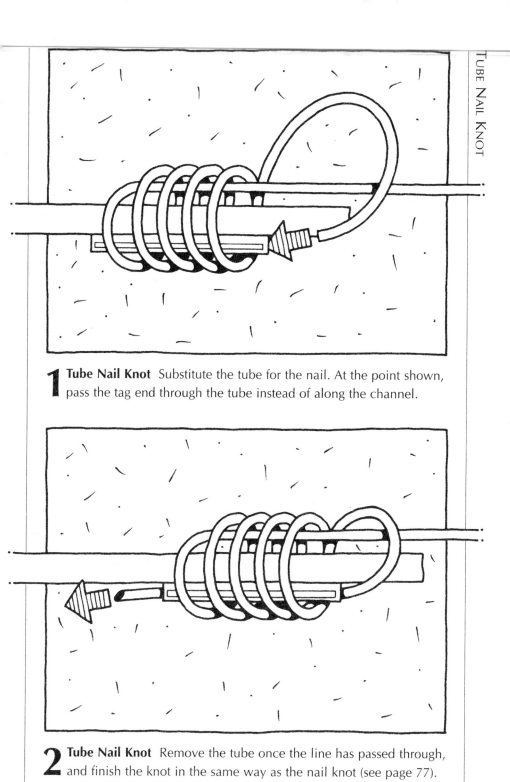

1 **Tube Nail Knot** Substitute the tube for the nail. At the point shown, pass the tag end through the tube instead of along the channel.

2 **Tube Nail Knot** Remove the tube once the line has passed through, and finish the knot in the same way as the nail knot (see page 77).

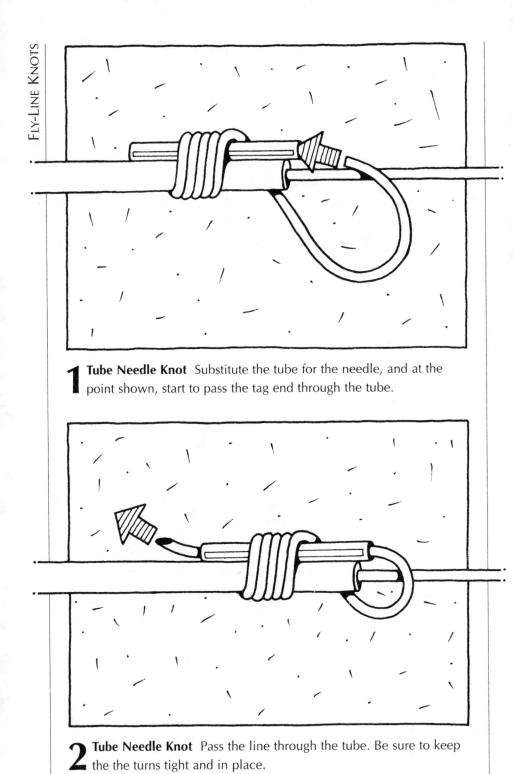

1 **Tube Needle Knot** Substitute the tube for the needle, and at the point shown, start to pass the tag end through the tube.

2 **Tube Needle Knot** Pass the line through the tube. Be sure to keep the the turns tight and in place.

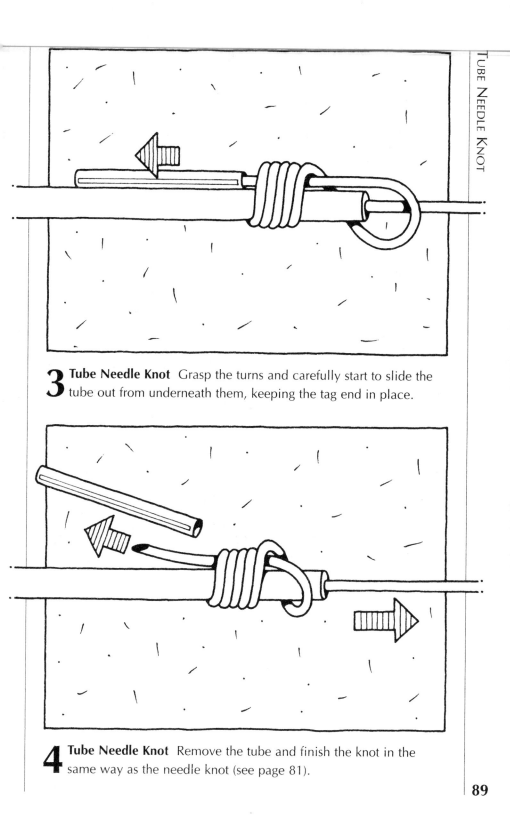

3 **Tube Needle Knot** Grasp the turns and carefully start to slide the tube out from underneath them, keeping the tag end in place.

4 **Tube Needle Knot** Remove the tube and finish the knot in the same way as the needle knot (see page 81).

EMERGENCY NAIL KNOT

If your nail or needle knot breaks while you are fishing, it is possible to solve the problem by creating an emergency nail knot with a strong piece of monofilament.

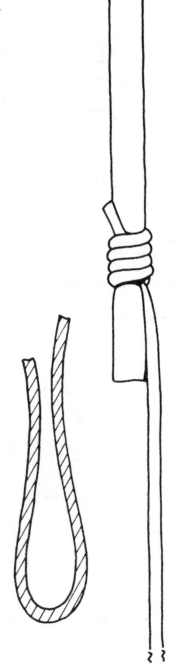

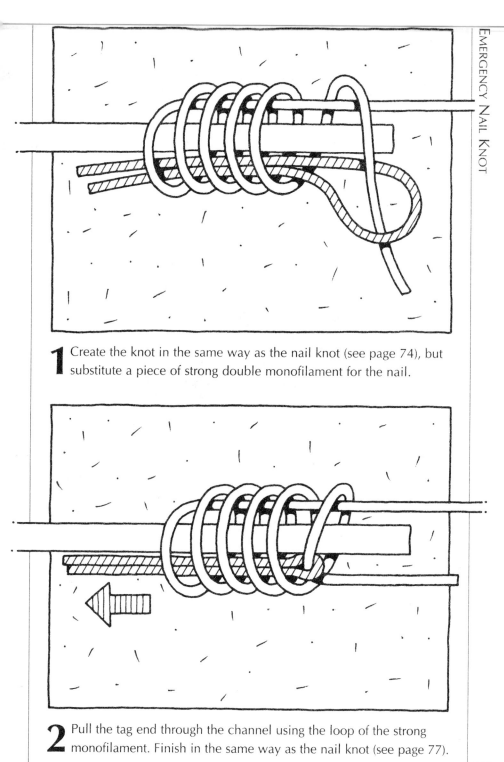

1 Create the knot in the same way as the nail knot (see page 74), but substitute a piece of strong double monofilament for the nail.

2 Pull the tag end through the channel using the loop of the strong monofilament. Finish in the same way as the nail knot (see page 77).

5
BOAT KNOTS

And finally, three secure boat knots. Many anglers fish from boats, and it is always useful to know the correct knots for tying up your craft.

Although these knots are referred to as "boat knots," like all knots they can have endless applications. For example, the quick-release knot (see page 100) can be used for any type of temporary fastening—from tying up your boat to tying up your dog!

PILE HITCH

This very neat and practical
knot is ideal for a temporary
mooring. Its big advantage is
that you can tie and untie
it very quickly.

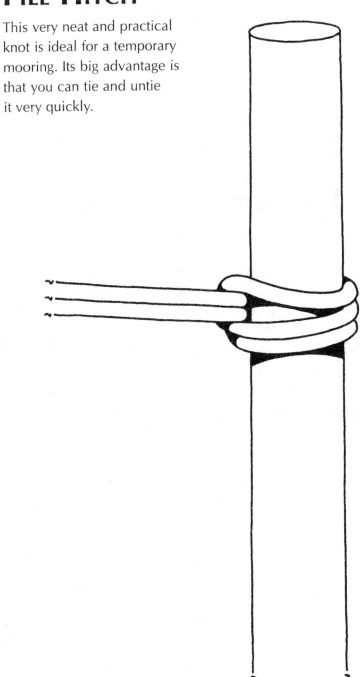

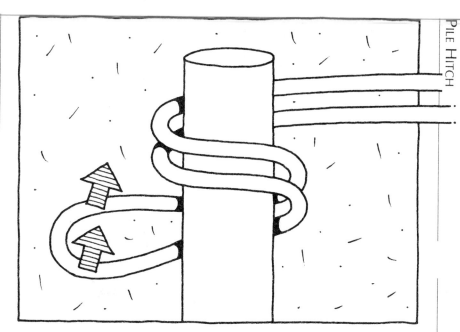

1 Double the end section of a rope and wrap it around a mooring post, leaving a loop big enough to pull back over the post.

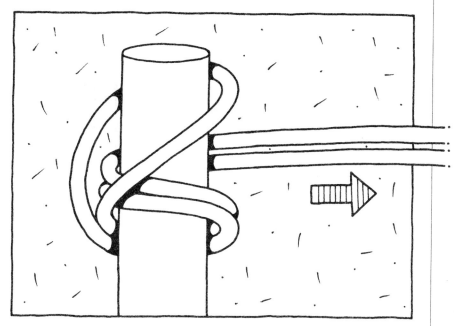

2 Pull the loop over the top of the post, and then pull on the standing part to tighten and secure the knot.

ANCHOR BEND

This knot is one of the most secure and widely used hitches for securing a boat to a ring or mooring post. It can also, as its name suggests, be used for tying to an anchor ring. For extra safety, a stopper knot can be added in the form of an additional half hitch.

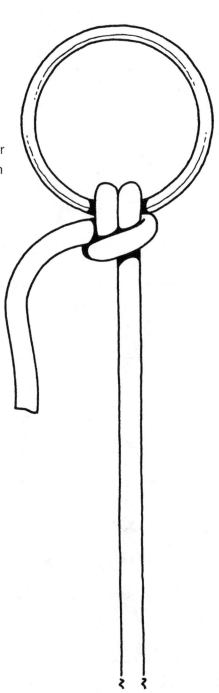

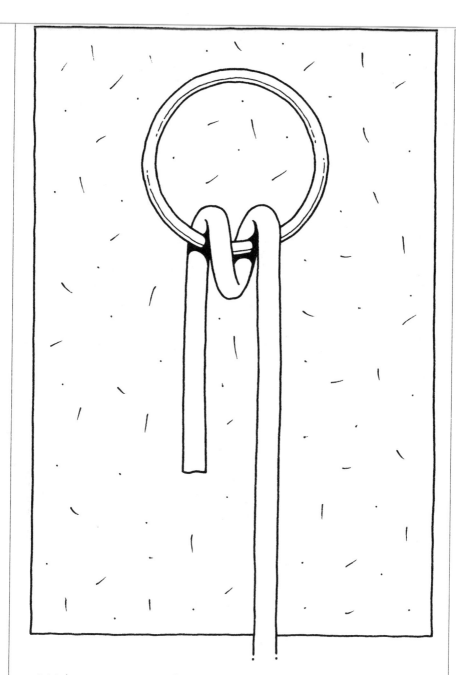

1 Make two turns around the ring with the tag end of the rope, as shown above.

2 Bring the tag end around the standing part and through the lower part of the turn.

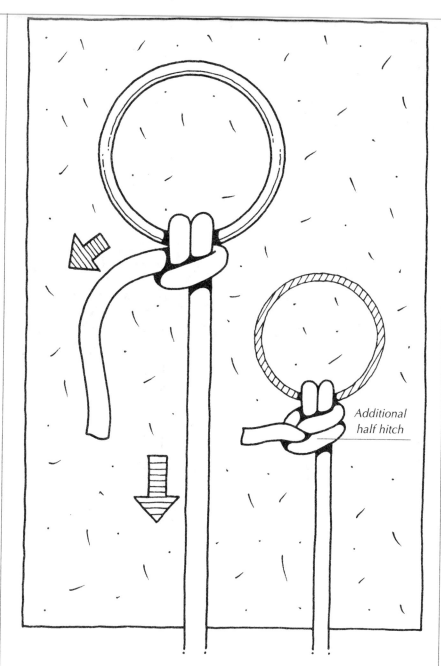

Additional half hitch

3 Pull on the tag end and standing part until the knot is secure.
At this point, an additional half hitch can be added for extra security.

QUICK-RELEASE KNOT

This extremely useful knot, also known as the **draw hitch,** can be used in any situation that requires a quick release. The standing part can be put under great tension—but with one pull on the tag end, the knot is undone.

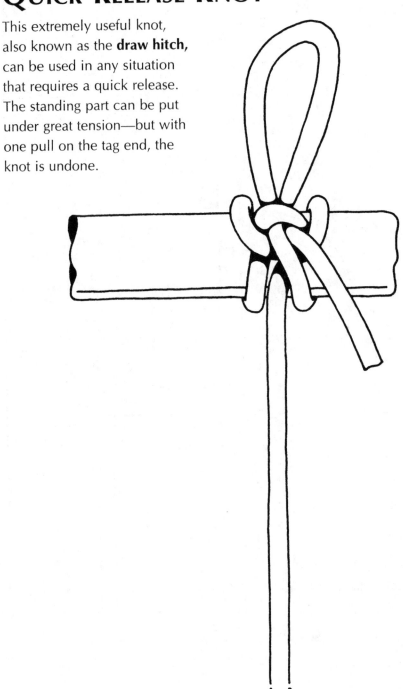

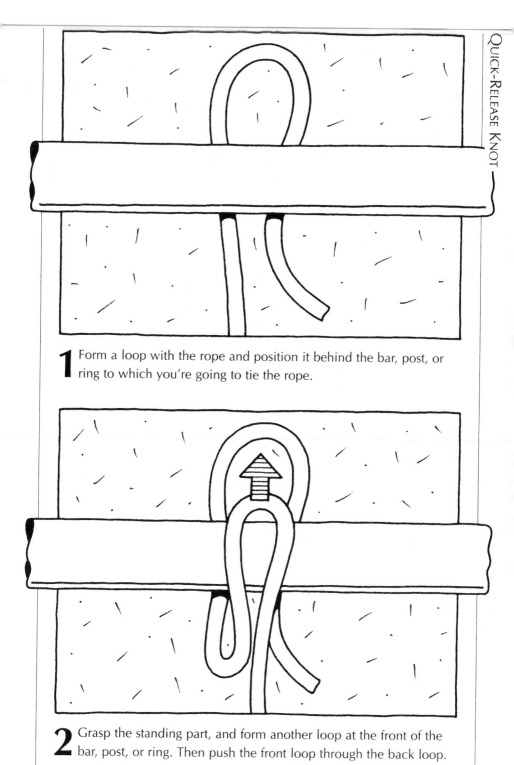

1 Form a loop with the rope and position it behind the bar, post, or ring to which you're going to tie the rope.

2 Grasp the standing part, and form another loop at the front of the bar, post, or ring. Then push the front loop through the back loop.

3 Pull the rear loop tight by pulling on the tag end. Then bring the tag end around to the front.

4 Grasp the tag end and form a third loop. This loop is now pushed through the remaining loop.

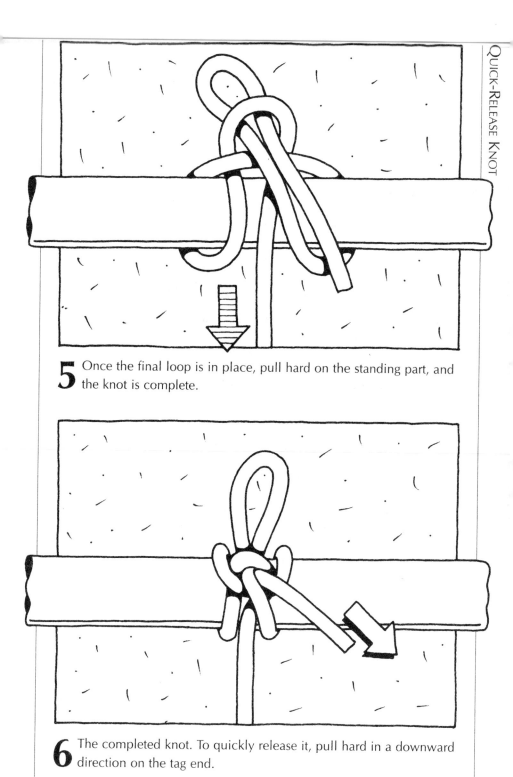

5 Once the final loop is in place, pull hard on the standing part, and the knot is complete.

6 The completed knot. To quickly release it, pull hard in a downward direction on the tag end.

GLOSSARY

Arbor The center of a reel spool.

Backing line High-breaking-strain monofilament or braided line used under the fly line on a reel to bulk out the spool. Also used as additional line when the fly line is stripped off the reel by a fish making a long run.

Bite Detection A rough measure of the sensitivity of a line by how clearly it communicates a fish's strike to the rod and hand; affected greatly by the stretch factor of a fishing line.

Braided line Line manufactured by interweaving several strands of material.

Breaking strength or strain the manufacture's estimate of the load that will cause the line to break. The calculation takes no account of wetness, wear and tear, knots, or shock loading.

Butt the thicker part of a leader, usually monofilament, that is attached to the fly line.

Copolymer A product of copolymerization, a chemical process by which two or more monomers (monofilaments) are combined to create a copolymer; sometimes a single monofilament sheathed entirely within another.

Dropper Short length of monofilament that is joined or tied into the leader to attach additional flies or tackle.

Eye A circle or loop attached or formed at the end of a hook or item of tackle, to which line is attached.

Fluorocarbon Line manufactured from extruded polyvinylidene fluoride that is non-porous, denser than water, and susceptible to very little stretch.

Fly line A coate nylon, Dacron, or PVC line specifically developed to cast an artificial fly attached to a leader.

Lanyard Short length of cord, often decorated, to secure objects or tackle; usually worn around the neck or attached to a belt.

Leader The tapered length of nylon that forms the connection between a fly line and a fly. It may be tapered mechanically (knotless), or created by joining sections of line with reducing diameters.

Line A term used to describe all types of fishing line.

Loop Part of the line that is bent to come together or cross itself.

Lure A term to describe artificial baits.

Monofilament Strong and flexible single-strand nylon line.

Recractor A spring-loaded spool of cord, usually pinned to clothing, to attach items such as scissors.

Seat/Seated A term used to describe the process of knot formation.

Shank The straight part of a hook.

Sinker Any weight, usually lead, that is attached to a fishing line.

Snell To tie a hook by wrapping line around the shank or straight part of the hook.

Spade end The flattened end of athe shank of a hook.

Standing part The main part of the line, usually not used in the actual tying of the knot.

Stopper knot Any terminal knot used at the end of line, usually to provide extra security.

Swivel An item of tackle used in the terminal rig to prevent twists of the line.

Tag end The part of the line in which the knot is tied and then the excess trimmed off.

Tippet The thin terminal section of th eleader, to which the fly is tied.

Turn One complete revolution of one line around another.

Conversion Chart

Note: These conversion factors are not exact. They are given only to the accuracy you're likely to need in everyday calculations.

Linear Measure

0.25 inch	= 0.6 cm
0.5 inch	= 1.25 cm
1 inch	= 2.54 cm
2 inches	= 5.08 cm
4 inches	= 10.16 cm
6 inches	= 15.25 cm
8 inches	= 20.32 cm
10 inches	= 25.40 cm
12 inches (1 foot)	= 30.48 cm
2 feet	= 0.61 m
3 feet (1 yard)	= 0.91 m
5 feet	= 1.52 m
10 feet	= 3.05 m

Measures of Weight

1 lb	= 450 g
2 lb	= 900 g
5 lb	= 2.25 kg
10 lb	= 4.5 kg
20 lb	= 9 kg
50 lb	= 23 kg
100 lb	= 46 kg

Temperature

Celsius	Fahrenheit
-17.8°	= 0°
-10°	= 14°
0°	= 32°
10°	= 50°
20°	= 68°
30°	= 86°
40°	= 104°
50°	= 122°
60°	= 140°
70°	= 158°
80°	= 176°
90°	= 194°
100°	= 212°

INDEX OF KNOTS